Google Pixel 9 Pro User Guide

Setup, Features, Customization, Troubleshooting, and Maximizing Your Smartphone Experience

By

Liam Vector

Disclaimer

This book is an independent, third-party user guide for the **Google Pixel 9 Pro**. It is not endorsed, authorized, or affiliated with **Google LLC** or any of its subsidiaries. The information provided within this guide is for educational purposes only and is intended to assist users in getting the most out of their Google Pixel 9 Pro device.

This guide does not aim to promote or advertise the **Google Pixel 9 Pro** or any other Google products or services. The views and opinions expressed in this book are those of the author and are not influenced by any corporate entity.

While every effort has been made to ensure the accuracy and reliability of the information provided, the author and publisher make no guarantees or warranties regarding the accuracy or completeness of the content. Users should refer to the official Google website or support resources for the most up-to-date and official product information.

Table of Contents

Introduction

- Welcome to the Google Pixel 9 Pro
- Key Features Overview
- How to Use This Guide

Chapter One: Getting Started

- Unboxing Your Google Pixel 9 Pro
- Powering On and Initial Setup
- Connecting to Wi-Fi and Google Account
- Setting Up Security (Face Unlock, Fingerprint)
- Transferring Data from Your Old Device

Chapter Two: Exploring the Display and Interface

- Overview of the 6.3-inch LTPO OLED Display
- Navigating the Home Screen and App Drawer
- Customizing the Home Screen and Widgets
- Understanding the 120Hz Refresh Rate

Chapter Three: Mastering the Camera System

- Overview of the Triple Camera Setup
  - 50 MP Wide, 48 MP Ultra-Wide, 48 MP Telephoto
- Using Portrait Mode, Night Sight, and Super Res Zoom
- Video Capture: 4K and 8K Options
- Camera AI Features: Photo Enhancement and Editing
- Front Camera Features and Best Practices

Chapter Four: Optimizing Performance

- Google Tensor G4 Processor and Memory Management
- Storage Management and Expansion Options
- Battery Life: Charging, Power Saving, and Battery Health
- Software Updates and Security Patches

Chapter Five: Customizing Your Pixel 9 Pro

- Display Settings: Brightness, Color, and Dark Mode
- Sounds and Notifications
- Setting Up Themes, Wallpapers, and Home Screen Customizations
- Configuring Gesture Controls

Chapter Six: Navigating Android 14 Features

- New Features in Android 14
- Setting Up Digital Wellbeing and Focus Mode
- Managing App Permissions and Privacy Settings
- Understanding and Using Google Assistant
- Mastering the Settings Menu and Quick Settings

Chapter Seven: AI Features and Integration

- Introduction to Gemini AI
- Using AI for Text Predictions, Photo Editing, and More
- Google One AI Premium Plan Features
- Smart Suggestions and Recommendations

Chapter Eight: Connectivity and Communication

- Connecting to Wi-Fi, Bluetooth, and NFC
- Using Google Meet and Google Messages
- Managing Dual SIM and eSIM
- Using Satellite SOS for Emergency Texts (U.S. Only)

Chapter Nine: Security and Privacy

- Setting Up Fingerprint and Face Unlock
- Two-Step Verification and Google Account Security
- Privacy Settings and Data Encryption
- Managing App Permissions and Location Services

Chapter Ten: Advanced Features and Tips

- Hidden Features and Customization Options
- Advanced Camera Tips (Super Res Zoom, AI Tools)
- Maximizing Battery and Performance
- Using Google Lens and Live Translate

Chapter Eleven: Troubleshooting and FAQs

- Resolving Common Issues (Wi-Fi, Bluetooth, Camera)
- Restoring Your Device to Factory Settings
- Solving Battery and Charging Issues
- Answering Frequently Asked Questions

Chapter Twelve: Accessories and Maintenance

- Recommended Accessories for Your Pixel 9 Pro
- Caring for Your Device: Case, Screen Protector, and Cleaning
- Software and Hardware Maintenance Tips
- Getting the Most Out of Google Support

Conclusion

- Summary of Key Features and Tips
- Where to Get Additional Help and Support
- Enjoying Your Pixel 9 Pro Experience

Introduction

Welcome to the Google Pixel 9 Pro

Welcome! You've just gotten your hands on the **Google Pixel 9 Pro**, one of the best smartphones Google has ever made. Whether you're new to smartphones or upgrading from a previous model, you'll find that the **Pixel 9 Pro** offers a smooth experience that can help you with everyday tasks and make your life easier in many ways.

This phone is designed to be simple to use while giving you access to powerful features like a great camera, fast internet, and helpful AI tools. With this guide, you will learn how to set up your new phone, use all of its features, and keep it running smoothly. Whether you want to take stunning photos, use Google Assistant, or explore the advanced settings, this guide will cover it all.

By the end of this book, you will feel comfortable using your **Google Pixel 9 Pro** and enjoy everything it has to offer. We'll guide you through the steps to help you get the most out of your phone.

Key Features Overview

The **Google Pixel 9 Pro** is built with **cutting-edge technology** that helps make your life easier. Here's a brief overview of some of its most exciting features:

1. **Camera Quality**: The camera on the **Pixel 9 Pro** is one of its strongest features. With three different lenses (wide, ultra-wide, and telephoto), you can take stunning photos, whether you're in bright sunlight or low-light environments. The phone uses AI to improve your pictures, making them look even better.

2. **Performance**: Inside the **Pixel 9 Pro**, there's a powerful processor that helps your phone run fast. You can quickly open apps, play games, and switch between tasks without lag. Whether you're at home or on the go, your phone will work smoothly.

3. **Battery Life**: The **Pixel 9 Pro** comes with a large battery that can last a full day with normal use. And if you need a quick boost, you can charge it quickly using the 27W fast charger that comes in the box. You'll also be able to charge wirelessly or even charge other devices if you need to.

4. **Google AI**: The **Pixel 9 Pro** uses Google's **AI** (artificial intelligence) to make your life easier. For example, Google Assistant can help you with voice commands like setting reminders, sending messages, or asking questions. The camera also

uses AI to improve photos and make them look even better.

5. **Display**: The phone has a beautiful **6.3-inch OLED display**. This means you'll see rich colors and sharp details, whether you're watching videos, browsing the internet, or looking at pictures. The screen refreshes at 120Hz, making it smoother to scroll and swipe.

6. **Security**: The **Pixel 9 Pro** comes with multiple ways to keep your phone safe. You can use **Face Unlock** or **Fingerprint Unlock** to protect your personal information. Google also includes a **Titan M2 security chip** for added safety.

7. **Software**: The phone runs **Android 14**, which is the latest version of Android. This means you'll get the newest features, security updates, and improvements. You'll also be able to use all of Google's apps, including Gmail, Google Photos, Google Maps, and many more.

How to Use This Guide

This guide is written to help you get the most out of your **Google Pixel 9 Pro**. It is organized into easy-to-follow chapters that will cover the basics of setting up your phone, using its features, and troubleshooting any problems. Here's how to use this guide:

1. **Start from the Beginning**: If you've just taken your phone out of the box, start with the first chapter. This will guide you through the **initial setup** process, including connecting to Wi-Fi and signing into your Google account.

2. **Read by Feature**: Each chapter focuses on a different feature of the **Pixel 9 Pro**. For example, if you want to learn about the **camera** in detail, head straight to the chapter on **Mastering the Camera System**. You'll find easy instructions for taking great photos and videos, even if you've never used a phone camera before.

3. **Take Your Time**: Don't feel rushed! Feel free to go back and reread any chapter. If you're unsure about something, come back to it later. There's no rush to learn everything at once.

4. **Refer Back to the Table of Contents**: The **Table of Contents** at the beginning of this book lists all the chapters. If you need information on something specific, like how to change the wallpaper or how to set up a password, you can find it easily by looking at the table of contents.

5. **Make Notes**: As you go through the guide, take notes on things that you find important or

interesting. The **Pixel 9 Pro** has many advanced features, so making notes will help you remember them as you continue to use your phone.

6. **Troubleshooting and FAQs**: If you run into any issues, refer to the **Troubleshooting** chapter. This chapter will help you fix common problems, such as when your phone won't connect to Wi-Fi or when apps aren't loading properly. We also have a **Frequently Asked Questions (FAQ)** section that can help answer any quick questions.

How This Guide Will Help You

The goal of this guide is simple: to help you become an expert at using your **Google Pixel 9 Pro**. Whether you are a first-time smartphone user or an experienced Android fan, this guide will provide all the information you need.

- **Easy Setup**: With simple, step-by-step instructions, we'll help you set up your phone in no time.
- **Use the Camera Like a Pro**: The **Pixel 9 Pro** has an amazing camera, and we'll show you how

to take great photos, adjust settings, and make your pictures look perfect.

- **Customize Your Experience**: Learn how to personalize your phone by changing the display, organizing apps, and setting up your home screen to match your style.
- **Troubleshoot Like a Pro**: If something goes wrong, we'll show you how to quickly solve common problems without getting frustrated.
- **Keep Your Phone Secure**: Your **Pixel 9 Pro** has many built-in features to keep your data safe. We'll explain how to set up security measures like Face Unlock, Fingerprint Unlock, and more.

Conclusion of the Introduction

The **Google Pixel 9 Pro** is more than just a phone; it's a tool that can help you stay connected, productive, and creative. With this guide, you'll have all the information you need to make the most of your new device. Whether you're capturing beautiful photos, using Google Assistant to make your life easier, or exploring the many features Android offers, we're here to help you every step of the way.

Chapter One

Getting Started

Welcome to the Google Pixel 9 Pro! This chapter will help you set up your new phone and get it ready for use. Don't worry, we will guide you step by step through the entire process. Whether this is your first smartphone or you've used others before, you will find that setting up your Pixel 9 Pro is simple and quick.

Let's begin with unboxing your new phone.

Unbox the Device

When you open the box for the first time, you will find several items inside. Make sure you have everything you need:

1. **Google Pixel 9 Pro Phone**:

    ○ This is the main device you've purchased. It will be wrapped in a protective layer to keep it safe during shipping.
    ○ Gently remove the phone from the box and set it aside on a flat surface, making sure not to drop it.

2. **Charger and Cable**:

   - You'll see a **USB-C to USB-C** cable inside the box. This cable is used for charging your phone and transferring data between your device and other devices like a computer.
   - The **fast charger** will allow you to charge your phone quickly. The Pixel 9 Pro supports **27W fast charging**, which can charge your device up to 50% in just about 30 minutes. Keep this charger handy for when you need to power up.

3. **SIM Ejector Tool**:

   - Inside the box, you'll also find a small tool. This is the **SIM ejector tool**, which is used to remove the SIM card tray from the side of your phone.
   - You'll need this tool to insert or remove your **SIM card**, which gives your phone access to mobile networks.

4. **User Manual**:

   - A small booklet with instructions on using your Google Pixel 9 Pro will also be included. While most of the steps will be in this guide, the manual will have some basic information as well, just in case you need to refer to it.

Once you've checked that all the contents are in the box, carefully place everything back inside so that it stays safe. You'll be able to use the SIM ejector tool in the next steps to insert your SIM card.

Powering On the Device

Now that you've unboxed your **Google Pixel 9 Pro**, it's time to power it on and begin the setup.

1. **Locate the Power Button**:

    ○ The **power button** is located on the right side of your phone. It's usually at the top, near the volume buttons. It's a long button that you can easily feel with your finger.

2. **Press and Hold the Power Button**:

    ○ To turn on the phone, press and hold the power button for a few seconds. You will see the **Google logo** appear on the screen. This means the phone is starting up. Be patient, as it might take a minute for the phone to fully turn on.

3. **Initial Setup Screen**:

    ○ Once the phone is powered on, you'll see the first setup screen. The device will ask

you to select your **language**. Use the
on-screen instructions to choose the
language you prefer.

Connecting to Wi-Fi

After selecting your language, the phone will guide you
to connect to a Wi-Fi network. Wi-Fi is important
because it allows you to access the internet without
using your mobile data.

1. **Choose Your Wi-Fi Network**:

    ○ You will see a list of Wi-Fi networks
       around you. Select the **Wi-Fi network**
       you want to connect to.
2. **Enter the Password**:

    ○ Once you've selected your Wi-Fi, it will
       ask you for the **password**. Type in your
       Wi-Fi password carefully. Remember,
       passwords are case-sensitive, so make
       sure you type it exactly as it appears.
3. **Connecting to Wi-Fi**:

    ○ After entering the password, press
       Connect. Your phone will connect to the
       Wi-Fi, and you should see a message

that says "Connected to [network name]."
This means you're ready to continue.

Signing Into Google Account

The next step is to sign into your **Google Account**. If
you already have a Google Account (for Gmail,
YouTube, or Google Photos), you can use it here.

1. **Sign In with Your Google Account**:

    o   On the next screen, you'll be asked to
        sign in. Enter your **email address** and
        password for your Google Account. If
        you don't have a Google Account, you
        can create a new one by selecting
        "Create Account" and following the steps.
2. **Sync Your Data**:

    o   Signing in will allow the phone to sync
        with your **Google services**, such as
        Gmail, Google Calendar, and Google
        Photos. This is how your contacts and
        emails will automatically appear on your
        phone.

Setting Up Security

To keep your phone safe, **Google Pixel 9 Pro** offers several options for **security**. It's important to choose a method for securing your device.

1. **Face Unlock**:

   - The **Face Unlock** feature allows you to unlock your phone by simply looking at it. To set it up, tap **Set Up Face Unlock** and follow the instructions on the screen. You'll need to position your face inside a frame and move your head slightly to help the phone get a good scan of your face.

2. **Fingerprint Unlock**:

   - Alternatively, you can set up **Fingerprint Unlock**. Go to **Settings > Security > Fingerprint**. Place your finger on the **under-display fingerprint sensor**, and the phone will scan and store your fingerprint. You may need to repeat this process a few times to ensure the phone captures a good scan of your fingerprint.

3. **Choose a Backup Lock Option**:

   - It's a good idea to have a **backup lock** option in case Face Unlock or Fingerprint Unlock doesn't work. You can set up a **PIN**, **Pattern**, or **Password** as your backup lock.

Inserting the SIM Card

To make calls and use mobile data, you'll need to insert your **SIM card**.

1. **Locate the SIM Tray**:

   ○ On the right side of your phone, you'll see a small **SIM tray**. This is where your SIM card goes. You will need the **SIM ejector tool** to open this tray.

2. **Use the SIM Ejector Tool**:

   ○ Insert the **SIM ejector tool** into the small hole near the tray. Press gently, and the tray will pop out.

3. **Insert the SIM Card**:

   ○ Place your **SIM card** into the tray. Make sure the metal part of the SIM card is facing down and the notched corner fits correctly in the tray. Once the SIM is properly placed, carefully slide the tray back into the phone.

Completing the Setup

Now that your phone is connected to Wi-Fi, your Google Account is set up, and the security options are in place, your **Google Pixel 9 Pro** is ready for use.

1. **Update Your Phone**:

   - It's important to check for any **software updates**. Go to **Settings > System > Software Update**. If an update is available, follow the on-screen instructions to install it.

2. **Restoring Data**:

   - If you have a backup from a previous device, your phone will ask if you want to restore your apps, photos, contacts, and settings from the backup. Choose **Restore** to bring everything over from your old phone.

3. **Set Up Google Services**:

   - You'll also be prompted to enable some of Google's services, such as **Google Backup**, **Location Services**, and **Google Assistant**. These services help your phone function smoothly and make your experience better.

4. **Customize Your Phone**:

   - Now that everything is set up, you can start customizing your phone. Change the

wallpaper, set up apps, and adjust
settings to fit your preferences.

Conclusion

Congratulations! Your **Google Pixel 9 Pro** is now set up
and ready to go. You can start exploring the many
features, apps, and tools the phone offers. In the next
chapters, we'll dive deeper into using the camera,
customizing the phone, and exploring all the amazing
things your new Pixel 9 Pro can do.

Take your time, and don't hesitate to come back to this
chapter if you need to review any steps. Enjoy your new
phone!

Powering On Your Google Pixel 9 Pro

Your **Google Pixel 9 Pro** is a powerful device with many
amazing features. However, before you can start
exploring all these features, the first step is to turn it on.
Let's walk through this process slowly and carefully.
We'll go step by step to make sure you understand how
to power on your new phone.

Step 1: Find the Power Button

The **power button** is a small, easy-to-find button located on the right side of your **Pixel 9 Pro**. It is usually near the middle of the right edge of the phone. This button is used for several purposes: it turns your phone on and off, locks and unlocks the screen, and allows you to restart the phone if needed.

- **Tip**: The power button is not on the top or bottom of the phone. It is located on the right side, slightly above the center.

Step 2: Press and Hold the Power Button

Now that you've located the power button, the next step is to **press and hold** it for a few seconds.

- To do this:
  1. **Press** the power button gently with your finger.
  2. **Hold** the button down for about **3-4 seconds**.

You should see the screen light up, and the **Google logo** will appear. If you do not see the logo right away, don't worry. Keep holding the button down, and the phone will start to boot up.

- **Why do we press and hold?**: Pressing and holding the power button for a few seconds tells the phone to wake up and start working. If you simply tap the button quickly, the phone might not turn on.

Step 3: Wait for the Phone to Boot Up

After holding the power button for a few seconds, you will see the **Google logo** appear on the screen. This means that your phone is starting to power on. The logo will be displayed for a short time, and then the phone will begin to load the operating system (the software that makes the phone work).

- **Tip**: If your phone is new, it may take a minute or two for the phone to fully start. This is normal. You don't need to press any more buttons; just wait and let the phone do its job.

You might see a loading symbol or animation as the phone prepares everything. Once it finishes loading, the **Welcome Screen** will appear, which means the phone is ready for the next steps in the setup process.

Step 4: What to Do if the Phone Doesn't Turn On

Sometimes, a phone might not turn on right away. If that happens, here are a few things you can try:

1. **Check the Battery**:
   If your phone doesn't turn on after you've pressed and held the power button, it may not have enough battery power. Plug your phone into the charger and leave it for about **15-20 minutes**. After some time, try pressing the power button again. The phone should start up now.

2. **Hard Reset**:
   If the phone still doesn't turn on, you may want to try a **hard reset**. This is done by pressing and holding the **power button** and the **volume down button** at the same time. Hold both buttons for about **10-15 seconds**. The phone should restart, and you will see the Google logo again.

3. **Contact Support**:
   If the phone still refuses to turn on, there could be an issue with the phone's hardware. In that case, contact **Google Support** or visit a **Google Store** to get further assistance.

Step 5: What Happens After the Phone Powers On

Once your phone is fully powered on and has finished booting up, you will see the **Welcome Screen**. This is where the fun really begins! The phone will ask you to select your **language** and will guide you through the **setup process**.

Here's what will happen next:

1. **Language Selection**:
   The first screen you see will ask you to select your preferred language. You can choose from many languages, such as English, Spanish, French, and more. Simply tap on the language

you want to use and press **Next**.

2. **Wi-Fi Connection**:
   After selecting your language, the phone will prompt you to connect to a **Wi-Fi network**. It will show you a list of available networks in your area. Tap on the one you want to connect to, enter the password (if needed), and then tap **Connect**.

3. **Sign In to Google Account**:
   The next screen will ask you to sign in with your **Google Account**. This step is important because it will allow you to access apps like **Gmail**, **Google Photos**, and **Google Maps**. If you don't have a Google Account, you can create one by following the instructions on the screen.

4. **Security Setup**:
   You'll then be prompted to set up **security options**, such as **Face Unlock** or **Fingerprint Unlock**, to keep your phone safe.

5. **Finish Setup**:
   Once you've completed all the setup steps, you'll be ready to start using your phone! You can start exploring all the features and apps that come with the **Google Pixel 9 Pro**.

What if You Need to Turn Off the Phone?

Now that you know how to turn your **Google Pixel 9 Pro** on, you may be wondering how to turn it off.

To turn off your phone:

1. **Press and hold the power button** (just like you did to turn it on).
2. A menu will appear on the screen with options to **Power Off** or **Restart**.
3. Tap **Power Off** to turn the phone off completely.

If you need to turn the phone back on, simply press and hold the **power button** again.

Conclusion

Turning on your **Google Pixel 9 Pro** is a simple process that begins with pressing and holding the power button for a few seconds. Once the phone powers up, you'll see the Google logo and be guided through the setup process. This guide walked you through the basic steps to get your phone up and running.

If you ever run into issues, don't worry. The troubleshooting steps, like charging the phone or performing a hard reset, should help. And if needed, Google Support is always available to assist you.

By now, your phone is powered on, and you're ready to dive deeper into its features. In the next chapters, we'll walk you through setting up Wi-Fi, signing into your Google account, and customizing your **Google Pixel 9 Pro** to suit your needs.

Enjoy your new phone!

Initial Setup for Your Google Pixel 9 Pro

Now that your **Google Pixel 9 Pro** is powered on, it's time to begin setting up your phone. This process is simple and easy to follow. By the end of it, your phone will be ready to use, and you'll be able to enjoy all the features it has to offer. We will guide you through this process step by step.

Step 1: Select Your Language

The first thing you will need to do when setting up your **Pixel 9 Pro** is to choose the language you want to use.

1. **Language Selection**:
    - When your phone powers on, the **Welcome Screen** will appear.
    - The first thing the phone will ask you to do is select your preferred **language**.

o   You will see a list of languages on the screen. These can include **English**, **Spanish**, **French**, **German**, and many others.
2. **How to Choose Your Language**:

o   Scroll through the list of languages using the **touchscreen**.
o   When you find your language, tap on it to select it. This will set the phone to use that language for everything, including menus, settings, and notifications.
o   After selecting your language, press **Next** at the bottom of the screen to continue with the setup.

Step 2: Connect Your Wi-Fi

Now that you've selected your language, the next step is to connect your phone to a **Wi-Fi network**. Wi-Fi is a type of internet connection that allows your phone to connect to the internet, use apps, and send and receive data without using your mobile data.

1. **Why Wi-Fi is Important**:

o   Wi-Fi is needed for tasks like downloading apps, updating your phone's software, browsing the internet, and using most of the features on your phone.

- ○ Connecting to Wi-Fi will also help you avoid using too much of your mobile data, which could lead to extra charges from your phone provider.

2. **How to Connect to Wi-Fi**:

- ○ Once you reach the **Wi-Fi Setup** screen, you will see a list of available Wi-Fi networks around you.
- ○ These networks might include your home Wi-Fi, a coffee shop Wi-Fi, or a public network. Your phone will automatically search for and display any networks it can find.
- ○ Find your **home Wi-Fi** in the list and tap on it. If you don't see your network, make sure your Wi-Fi router is turned on, or try moving closer to the router.

3. **Entering the Wi-Fi Password**:

- ○ After selecting your Wi-Fi network, your phone will ask you to enter the **password** for the network.
- ○ **Wi-Fi passwords** are often case-sensitive, which means that **capital letters** and **small letters** must be typed exactly as they appear.
- ○ If you don't know your Wi-Fi password, you may need to check it on your Wi-Fi

router or ask the person who manages the Wi-Fi.

4. **Connecting**:

   ○ Once you've typed in the password correctly, tap **Connect**. Your phone will now connect to your Wi-Fi.
   ○ You should see a message that says **"Connected"** when your phone has successfully connected to the Wi-Fi network.
   ○ If your phone does not connect, double-check the password or try connecting to another Wi-Fi network.

5. **Why This Step is Important**:

   ○ Connecting to Wi-Fi is crucial for downloading updates, setting up apps, and using Google services.
   ○ Without a Wi-Fi connection, your phone might not be able to download everything needed to complete the setup, and you may run into issues later on.

Step 3: Sign In with Your Google Account

Your **Google Account** is very important because it gives you access to many of the services that come with your phone, such as **Gmail**, **Google Photos**, **Google**

Drive, and the **Google Play Store**. Signing in with your Google Account will allow you to back up your data, download apps, and sync your contacts and calendar.

1. **Why Signing in is Important**:

   - By signing in with your **Google Account**, you'll be able to access all the information you've saved in Google services, such as contacts, emails, and photos.
   - It also allows you to download apps from the **Google Play Store** and make use of Google's cloud services.

2. **How to Sign In with Your Google Account**:

   - After you connect to Wi-Fi, the phone will ask you to **sign in** to your **Google Account**.
   - If you already have a Google Account (for example, if you use **Gmail**, **YouTube**, or **Google Docs**), enter your **email address** and **password** to sign in.
   - If you don't have a Google Account, tap on **Create Account** and follow the instructions to set one up. You'll need to choose a username and password, and fill out some personal information.

3. **Google Services Setup**:

   - After you sign in, your phone will ask if you want to enable some **Google**

services, such as **Google Backup** (which saves your data), **Location Services** (which helps with maps and directions), and **Google Assistant** (a voice assistant that helps you with tasks).

- ○ You can choose to enable or skip each service depending on your preferences. You can always change these settings later.

4. **Syncing Data**:

- ○ Once you sign in, your phone will start syncing your **Google services**. This means that all the information you have stored with Google, such as emails, contacts, and calendar events, will automatically appear on your phone.
- ○ If you have previously used **Google Photos**, your pictures and videos will also sync and be available on your Pixel 9 Pro.

Step 4: Agreeing to Terms and Conditions

After signing in to your Google Account, the phone will ask you to agree to **Google's Terms of Service** and **Privacy Policy**. These are important agreements that tell you how Google will use your data and what they will do to protect your privacy.

1. **Read and Accept the Terms**:
    - You can tap on the links to **read** the full **Terms of Service** and **Privacy Policy**, but you can also choose to simply accept them if you agree.
    - Once you agree, your phone will proceed to the next setup step.

Step 5: Set Up Additional Services (Optional)

Now that your phone is connected to Wi-Fi and signed into your Google Account, you'll be prompted to set up some additional services. These are optional but can make your phone experience much better.

1. **Google Assistant**:

    - Google Assistant is a voice-controlled tool that can help you with many tasks. You can ask Google Assistant to set reminders, send texts, check the weather, and more.
    - To set it up, simply follow the on-screen instructions to activate Google Assistant. You'll be asked to say a few phrases so the phone can recognize your voice.
2. **Location Services**:

- ○ Location services help apps like **Google Maps** know where you are, so you can get directions, find local restaurants, and more.
- ○ You'll be asked if you want to enable **Location Services**. You can choose to turn it on or off based on your preferences. You can always adjust this later.

3. **Backup & Restore**:

- ○ If you've used a previous Android device, you'll have the option to **restore your data** from Google's cloud. This will bring over your apps, photos, contacts, and more.
- ○ If this is your first Android phone or you don't have a backup, don't worry – your phone will still work just fine. You can always set up backups in the future.

Step 6: Completing the Setup

Once you've gone through all the steps, your phone will finish setting up and be ready to use. You'll see the **Home Screen**, where you can begin customizing your phone, downloading apps, and exploring the features of the **Google Pixel 9 Pro**.

1. **Explore the Home Screen**:

   ○ The **Home Screen** is where you'll see your apps. Tap on any app icon to open it. You can customize the home screen by adding new apps or changing the wallpaper.

2. **Finish Customizing Your Phone**:

   ○ You can change the **wallpaper**, adjust the **display settings**, and add widgets to your home screen. To do this, tap and hold on an empty space on the home screen, and then select **Wallpaper** or **Widgets**.

Conclusion

You've now completed the initial setup for your **Google Pixel 9 Pro**. Your phone is connected to Wi-Fi, signed into your Google Account, and ready for use. You can start exploring all the features that make this phone so special. From taking pictures to navigating with **Google Maps** and using **Google Assistant**, the possibilities are endless.

Take your time to explore the features in this guide, and soon you'll be using your **Google Pixel 9 Pro** like a pro!

Setting Up Security on Your Google Pixel 9 Pro

In this chapter, we will guide you through setting up the security features on your **Google Pixel 9 Pro**. Keeping your phone secure is very important, as it holds a lot of personal information like your contacts, photos, and messages. Fortunately, your **Pixel 9 Pro** offers two ways to keep your phone safe: **Face Unlock** and **Fingerprint Unlock**.

These features are easy to set up and use, and we will explain each one in detail so you can choose the best option for you.

Why Security Is Important

Your **Google Pixel 9 Pro** is much more than just a phone. It holds a lot of your personal data, including your emails, photos, notes, and more. By setting up a security method, you make sure that no one else can easily access your personal information.

- **Face Unlock** allows you to unlock your phone just by looking at it. It's quick and easy, but it's important to set it up correctly to ensure it works well.

- **Fingerprint Unlock** is another option where you scan your finger to unlock the phone. It's very secure and also fast.

Now, let's go through the steps to set up both of these security options.

Setting Up Face Unlock

Face Unlock is a convenient and fast way to unlock your **Google Pixel 9 Pro**. It uses the front camera on your phone to scan your face and unlock the device. Here are the steps to set it up:

Step 1: Open the Settings App

1. To begin, go to the **Home Screen** and find the **Settings app**. The **Settings app** looks like a small gear icon.
2. Tap on the **Settings app** to open it.

Step 2: Go to Security Settings

1. In the **Settings** menu, scroll down until you find the option labeled **Security**. It is usually under the "Personal" section.
2. Tap on **Security** to open the security options for your phone.

Step 3: Select Face Unlock

1. Once you're in the **Security** menu, look for the option labeled **Face Unlock**.
2. Tap on **Face Unlock** to start the setup process.

Step 4: Confirm Your Lock Screen Method

Before you can set up **Face Unlock**, you need to have a secure lock screen set up. This means you need to have either a **PIN**, **Pattern**, or **Password** already in place.

1. If you haven't set up a lock screen, the phone will ask you to choose one. You can choose a **PIN**, **Pattern**, or **Password**. This is important for protecting your phone if Face Unlock doesn't work.
2. Choose the **PIN**, **Pattern**, or **Password** that works best for you. Follow the on-screen instructions to set it up.

Step 5: Scan Your Face

1. After confirming your lock screen method, the phone will ask you to **scan your face**.
2. To scan your face, the phone will show you a **frame** on the screen. Hold the phone in front of your face, ensuring your face is within the frame.
3. Move your head slowly in small circles so the camera can capture different angles of your face. This helps the phone get a more accurate scan.
4. Once the scan is complete, the phone will confirm that **Face Unlock** is set up.

Step 6: Test Face Unlock

1. To test if it works, lock your phone by pressing the **power button** once.
2. After a few seconds, press the **power button** again to wake up the phone.
3. Look at the phone, and the **Face Unlock** feature should recognize your face and unlock the phone immediately.

Step 7: Adjust Settings for Face Unlock

1. If you want to change or adjust your **Face Unlock** settings, go back to **Settings > Security > Face Unlock**.
2. Here, you can adjust settings like enabling **screen wake**, which means the phone will automatically wake up when you look at it.

Setting Up Fingerprint Unlock

Another secure and fast way to unlock your phone is using **Fingerprint Unlock**. This method uses the **fingerprint sensor** built into the **Pixel 9 Pro** to unlock your phone. Here's how you can set it up:

Step 1: Go to Security Settings

1. Like with **Face Unlock**, you need to start by opening the **Settings** app.

2. Scroll down to **Security** and tap it to open the security settings.

Step 2: Select Fingerprint

1. In the **Security** menu, you'll see an option called **Fingerprint**.
2. Tap on **Fingerprint** to begin the setup process.

Step 3: Set Up a Lock Screen (If You Haven't Already)

Before you can use **Fingerprint Unlock**, you need to have a lock screen set up for security.

1. If you haven't already set up a **PIN**, **Pattern**, or **Password**, the phone will ask you to do so. This is important because **Fingerprint Unlock** works together with your chosen lock screen method.
2. Choose a lock screen method and follow the instructions to set it up.

Step 4: Scan Your Fingerprint

1. After setting up your lock screen, the phone will prompt you to **scan your fingerprint**.
2. Place your **finger** (usually your **index finger**) on the **under-display fingerprint sensor** located on the **front of the phone**.
3. The phone will ask you to **lift and place your finger** on the sensor several times. Make sure to

place your finger in different positions to get a complete scan of your fingerprint.

Step 5: Complete the Setup

1. Once the phone has successfully scanned your fingerprint, it will confirm that the setup is complete.
2. You can now use your fingerprint to unlock your phone by placing your finger on the fingerprint sensor.

Step 6: Test Fingerprint Unlock

1. To test if **Fingerprint Unlock** works, press the **power button** to lock your phone.
2. After the phone is locked, press the **power button** again to wake it up.
3. Place your registered finger on the **fingerprint sensor**. The phone should immediately recognize your fingerprint and unlock.

Security Tips for Face Unlock and Fingerprint Unlock

Now that you've set up both **Face Unlock** and **Fingerprint Unlock**, here are some tips to help ensure that your phone remains secure:

1. **Make Sure the Camera is Clean**:
   For **Face Unlock** to work well, keep the **front camera** clean. Wipe it gently with a soft cloth if it gets dirty. This will help the phone read your face correctly.

2. **Add Multiple Fingerprints**:
   For **Fingerprint Unlock**, consider scanning more than one finger. For example, register your left and right hands so that you can unlock your phone with either hand, even if your phone is placed in different positions.

3. **Be Mindful of Lighting for Face Unlock**:
   Face Unlock works best in good lighting. If you are in a dark room, the camera may have trouble recognizing your face. Try to use **Face Unlock** in well-lit areas for the best experience.

4. **Backup Lock Method**:
   Always have a **backup lock method**, such as a **PIN**, **Pattern**, or **Password**, set up in case your **Face Unlock** or **Fingerprint Unlock** doesn't work. For example, if your fingers are wet or if you're in an area where **Face Unlock** has trouble, the backup method will help you unlock your phone.

5. **Security Enhancements**:
   In **Settings > Security**, you can enable **Smart Lock**. Smart Lock keeps your phone unlocked

when you're in trusted places, like at home, or when it recognizes a connected Bluetooth device, like your smartwatch.

Conclusion

Setting up **Face Unlock** and **Fingerprint Unlock** on your **Google Pixel 9 Pro** is simple and straightforward. These features make it easy for you to unlock your phone quickly and securely. Whether you choose to use **Face Unlock** or **Fingerprint Unlock**, or even both, these options help keep your phone and personal data safe.

By following the steps outlined in this chapter, you'll ensure that your **Google Pixel 9 Pro** remains secure and easy to access whenever you need it. Take a moment to set up these features, and your phone will be ready for anything you need.

Let's move on to the next chapters where we will dive deeper into using your **Pixel 9 Pro** to its full potential.

Transfer Data to Your Google Pixel 9 Pro

When you get a new phone, one of the first things you'll want to do is transfer all the data from your old phone to your new one. Whether you're upgrading from an old **Android phone** or switching from **iPhone**, the **Google Pixel 9 Pro** offers a simple way to move everything over so you don't lose any important information.

The process is straightforward, and you can do it in two ways: using the **Quick Switch Adapter** or restoring from a **Google Backup**. Let's go through each method, step by step.

Option 1: Using the Quick Switch Adapter

The **Quick Switch Adapter** is a small device included with your **Google Pixel 9 Pro**. This tool allows you to connect your old phone to your new one, so you can transfer all your data—contacts, messages, photos, and apps—without much effort.

Here's how to use it:

1. **Locate the Quick Switch Adapter**:

   ○ After unboxing your **Pixel 9 Pro**, you'll find the **Quick Switch Adapter** inside the box. It's a small adapter with two connectors: one for your **old phone** and one for your **new Pixel 9 Pro**.

2. **Plug in the Adapter**:

- First, take the **Quick Switch Adapter** and plug the **USB-C end** into your **Google Pixel 9 Pro**.
- Now, connect the other end of the adapter to your old phone. If your old phone uses a **USB-A** connector (like most older Android phones or iPhones), you may need a **USB-A to USB-C** cable, which can be plugged into the adapter.

3. **Turn on Both Phones**:

- Make sure both phones are turned on. Once connected, your **Google Pixel 9 Pro** will detect the old phone and prompt you to begin the transfer process.

4. **Select What to Transfer**:

- Your phone will now ask what you want to transfer from your old phone to the **Pixel 9 Pro**. You can choose things like:
    - Contacts
    - Photos and Videos
    - Apps
    - Messages
    - Music and Files
- You can select all or just specific items to transfer, depending on what you want to bring over from your old phone.

5. **Start the Transfer**:

- Once you've selected everything you want to transfer, tap **Next**. The **Pixel 9 Pro** will begin transferring the selected data from your old phone to your new device.
- The transfer process can take some time, especially if you have a lot of data to move. Make sure both phones are plugged in or have enough battery to finish the transfer.

6. **Finish the Transfer**:

- Once the data transfer is complete, your new **Pixel 9 Pro** will let you know. Now, all your important information will be on your new phone, and you can start using it right away.

Option 2: Restore from Google Backup

If you've been using **Google Backup** to save your data to the cloud, you can easily restore everything to your new **Pixel 9 Pro**. This method is especially useful if you've already set up Google services like Gmail and Google Photos on your old device. It's also a great option if you've lost or misplaced your Quick Switch Adapter.

Here's how to restore your data from **Google Backup**:

1. **Connect to Wi-Fi**:

   - Before you can restore from **Google Backup**, make sure your **Pixel 9 Pro** is connected to Wi-Fi. You can do this during the initial setup process if you haven't done it yet.

2. **Sign in to Your Google Account**:

   - When you sign in to your **Google Account** during setup, your phone will ask if you want to restore data from a backup. Tap **Restore** to begin the process.

3. **Select Your Backup**:

   - You will see a list of **backups** available. If you've backed up your data to **Google Drive**, it will show up here. Select the backup you want to restore from.
   - The list will show the date of the last backup, so you can choose the most recent one or another backup if needed.

4. **Choose What to Restore**:

   - After selecting the backup, the phone will ask what you want to restore. You can choose from:

- **Apps**: All the apps you had installed on your previous phone will be reinstalled automatically.
- **Contacts**: Your contacts saved to **Google Contacts** will be restored.
- **Photos and Videos**: Your **Google Photos** backup will be restored.
- **Messages**: Your text messages will be restored from **Google Backup**.
    - Select everything you want to restore, then tap **Next** to proceed.

5. **Wait for the Restore to Complete**:

    - The phone will begin restoring your data from the **Google Backup**. This process can take several minutes, depending on how much data you have.
    - While the restore is happening, you can continue with other setup tasks like setting up security, Wi-Fi, and Google services.

6. **Check Your Restored Data**:

    - Once the restore process is complete, you can open your apps, check your contacts, and see your photos in **Google Photos**.

- If you have any apps or data that didn't restore, you can manually install or restore them later.

Finish Setup

Once you've transferred your data and restored from **Google Backup**, you'll need to complete the final steps of the setup process to get your phone ready to use.

Step 1: Sync Your Apps

After transferring your data, you might want to sync your **apps** so they can be updated to the latest versions.

1. **Update Your Apps**:

   - Go to the **Google Play Store** to check for app updates. Open the **Play Store** app, tap the **Menu icon** (three lines in the top-left corner), then select **My apps & games**.
   - Tap **Update All** to update all your apps at once, or you can choose to update specific apps by tapping the **Update** button next to them.
2. **Enable Automatic App Updates**:

- To make sure your apps stay up-to-date in the future, go to **Settings > Google > Play Store** and enable the option for **Auto-update apps**.

Step 2: Sign into Additional Accounts

After restoring your apps and data, you might need to sign in to your other accounts, such as social media, email, or cloud storage.

1. **Sign into Your Email**:

   - If you use email accounts other than **Google**, like **Outlook** or **Yahoo**, you can set them up by going to **Settings > Accounts > Add Account**.
   - Follow the on-screen instructions to enter your username and password for your email accounts.

2. **Sign into Social Media Accounts**:

   - For social media apps like **Facebook**, **Instagram**, or **Twitter**, open the apps and sign in using your credentials.

3. **Set Up Cloud Storage**:

   - If you use cloud storage apps like **Dropbox** or **OneDrive**, open them and sign in with your account details to restore any files you might need.

Step 3: Enable Optional Features

Your **Google Pixel 9 Pro** offers a variety of optional features that you can enable to improve your experience. These features can help with security, navigation, and more.

1. **Enable Location Services**:

    o **Location services** allow your phone to use GPS to provide location-based services, like getting directions in **Google Maps**.
    o To enable this feature, go to **Settings > Location**, and make sure **Location** is turned on.

2. **Set Up Google Assistant**:

    o Google Assistant is a helpful feature that lets you control your phone and perform tasks using voice commands.
    o To set it up, go to **Settings > Google > Search, Assistant & Voice** and follow the instructions to enable **Google Assistant**.

3. **Enable Backup**:

    o Make sure that **Google Backup** is turned on to automatically back up your data, such as apps, photos, and messages.

- To enable backup, go to **Settings > System > Backup**, and toggle **Back up to Google Drive** to the **on** position.
4. **Customize Your Display**:

- You can change the **wallpaper**, adjust the **screen brightness**, and enable **Dark Mode** by going to **Settings > Display**.

Conclusion

You've now completed the **data transfer** and **setup** process for your **Google Pixel 9 Pro**. Your new phone is ready to use, and all your important data, apps, and settings are now in place.

By following these steps, you've successfully moved your information from your old phone, set up your Google services, and customized your phone to suit your needs. Enjoy exploring all the exciting features your **Pixel 9 Pro** has to offer, from the powerful camera to the sleek design and advanced AI capabilities.

Remember, if you ever need help, you can always return to the **Settings** menu to adjust anything or refer to this guide for assistance.

Chapter Two

Exploring the Display and Interface

In this chapter, we will take a closer look at the **Google Pixel 9 Pro**'s **display** and **interface**. The display is one of the most important features of your phone because it is where you see everything—your apps, photos, messages, and videos. The interface is how you interact with the phone, and it helps you navigate and use all the features smoothly.

Let's explore the different parts of the display and interface of your **Google Pixel 9 Pro**. We will also explain how to adjust the settings to make your experience more comfortable and personalized.

Understanding the Display

The **Google Pixel 9 Pro** comes with a **6.3-inch OLED display**. This means that the screen uses **OLED** (Organic Light Emitting Diode) technology, which allows for brighter, more vivid colors and deeper blacks compared to other types of screens. When you look at the screen, everything will appear clear, crisp, and vibrant.

OLED displays are known for their ability to show **true black colors**, meaning that when a part of the screen shows black, it actually turns off the pixels, creating a deep, dark black that looks great on the screen. This technology also helps save battery life because dark areas of the screen use less power.

Let's break down the features of the **Pixel 9 Pro's display** and show you how to adjust the settings.

---

1. Brightness

The brightness of your phone's display affects how easily you can see the screen in different lighting conditions. For example, in bright sunlight, you may want to increase the brightness to see the screen clearly. On the other hand, in a dark room, you may want to lower the brightness to avoid straining your eyes.

To adjust the brightness of the display on your **Google Pixel 9 Pro**, follow these steps:

1. **Swipe Down from the Top of the Screen**:

    o   Place your finger at the top of the screen and swipe it down. This will open the **Quick Settings** menu, where you can adjust the brightness.

2. **Use the Brightness Slider**:

    o   You will see a slider that allows you to adjust the brightness of the screen. Move the slider to the right to increase brightness or to the left to decrease brightness.

    o   **Tip**: In bright outdoor environments, you may want to set the brightness to the highest level. In darker settings, reduce the brightness to save battery and make the screen more comfortable to view.

3. **Automatic Brightness**:

    o   If you want your phone to automatically adjust the brightness based on your surroundings, you can turn on **Adaptive Brightness**. To enable this, go to **Settings > Display** and toggle on **Adaptive Brightness**. Your phone will then adjust the brightness based on the lighting conditions around you.

---

2. Color and Display Settings

The **Google Pixel 9 Pro** allows you to customize the color and appearance of the screen to suit your preferences. You can adjust the **color temperature** and **screen mode** to make the display look warmer or cooler depending on your liking.

To change the **color settings**, follow these steps:

1. **Go to Settings**:

   - Open the **Settings** app from your home screen or app drawer.

2. **Tap on Display**:

   - Scroll down in the **Settings** menu and tap on **Display**.

3. **Adjust the Screen Mode**:

   - In the **Display** section, you will find an option called **Screen Mode**. Here, you can choose between different modes like **Natural**, **Vivid**, or **Adaptive**. Each mode changes the color balance of the screen to make it look warmer, cooler, or more vivid. Choose the mode that looks best to you.

4. **Adjust the Color Temperature**:

   - If you want to change the overall warmth or coolness of the screen, tap on **Advanced** and then choose **Color**. You can then adjust the temperature by sliding the color slider to make the screen appear warmer (more yellow) or cooler (more blue).

---

3. Dark Mode

Dark Mode is a feature that changes the appearance of your phone's interface to a dark color scheme. Instead of bright white backgrounds, everything becomes darker, with black or dark gray backgrounds and lighter text. This can be easier on your eyes, especially in low-light conditions, and it can help save battery life because darker pixels use less power on an **OLED** display.

To enable **Dark Mode** on your **Google Pixel 9 Pro**, follow these steps:

1. **Go to Settings**:

   ○ Open the **Settings** app.
2. **Select Display**:

   ○ Scroll down and tap on **Display**.
3. **Tap on Dark Theme**:

   ○ Under the **Display** settings, you will see the **Dark Theme** option. Tap it to turn on **Dark Mode**.
4. **Schedule Dark Mode**:

○ If you prefer to use **Dark Mode** only at certain times (for example, at night), you can schedule it to turn on and off automatically. Tap on **Dark Theme**, and then select **Turn on at night** to set up a schedule.

Navigating the Interface

Now that you understand the display settings, let's look at how you interact with your **Google Pixel 9 Pro**. The **interface** refers to the way you interact with the phone using the screen and buttons. The **Pixel 9 Pro** uses **gestures** and **buttons** to help you navigate through apps, settings, and features.

---

1. Home Screen and App Drawer

The **Home Screen** is where you can find your apps, widgets, and shortcuts. You can customize your **Home Screen** by adding new apps, changing the wallpaper, and organizing the icons.

Here's how to use your **Home Screen** and **App Drawer**:

1. **Access the Home Screen:**

- When you turn on your phone, you will land on the **Home Screen**. The **Home Screen** is where all your apps are displayed.

2. **Organize Apps**:

   - To organize your apps, tap and hold on an app icon. This will allow you to move the app to a different position or create a folder by dragging one app onto another.

3. **Add Apps to the Home Screen**:

   - To add an app to the **Home Screen**, open the **App Drawer** (by swiping up from the bottom of the screen), then drag an app to the **Home Screen**.

4. **Change the Wallpaper**:

   - To change the wallpaper, tap and hold on an empty space on the **Home Screen**, and then select **Wallpapers**. You can choose a default wallpaper, a photo from your gallery, or download new wallpapers from the internet.

---

2. Using Gestures to Navigate

Your **Google Pixel 9 Pro** uses **gestures** to help you navigate the phone without buttons. This is an efficient way to move around and access apps quickly. If you are used to buttons, don't worry. You can also enable the **Navigation Bar** with the familiar home, back, and recent apps buttons.

To use **gestures**, follow these steps:

1. **Go to Settings**:

   - Open the **Settings** app.
2. **Tap on System**:

   - Scroll down and tap on **System**.
3. **Select Gestures**:

   - Tap on **Gestures** and choose the **Swipe gestures** option.
4. **Using Gestures**:

   - **Home Screen**: To go to the Home Screen, swipe up from the bottom of the screen.
   - **Back**: To go back, swipe from the left or right edge of the screen.
   - **Recent Apps**: To view your recent apps, swipe up from the bottom and hold for a moment.

You can also choose to enable the **Navigation Bar** if you prefer to use buttons. To do this, go to **Settings >**

System > Gestures > System Navigation, and select **3-button navigation**.

---

3. Quick Settings Menu

The **Quick Settings Menu** allows you to easily access important features like **Wi-Fi, Bluetooth, Do Not Disturb**, and **Battery Saver**. To open the **Quick Settings Menu**, simply swipe down from the top of the screen.

1. **Swipe Down from the Top**:

   ○ Place your finger at the top of the screen and swipe it down. This will open the **Quick Settings**.

2. **Adjust Settings**:

   ○ Here, you can quickly toggle settings like **Wi-Fi, Bluetooth, Airplane Mode, Brightness**, and **Volume**.

3. **More Settings**:

   ○ If you need more options, tap the **gear icon** to open the full **Settings** menu.

Conclusion

In this chapter, we've explored the key features of the **Google Pixel 9 Pro** display and interface. The **6.3-inch OLED display** provides vibrant colors and deep blacks, making everything you see look stunning. You've learned how to adjust the brightness, change the screen mode, and activate **Dark Mode**.

You also learned how to navigate your phone using **gestures** or the **Navigation Bar**, customize your **Home Screen**, and use the **Quick Settings Menu** for quick access to key features.

With this knowledge, you're ready to start using your **Google Pixel 9 Pro** to its fullest potential. In the next chapters, we will dive deeper into other features like the **camera system**, **performance**, and **security** to help you get the most out of your new device.

Navigating the Home Screen

The **Home Screen** is the main area on your phone where you can see all your apps, shortcuts, and widgets. It is the first screen you see when you turn on your phone and press the **Home Button** (or swipe up, depending on your settings).

Returning to the Home Screen

When you use your phone, you may open many apps, and sometimes you might want to go back to the **Home**

Screen. There are two ways to return to the **Home Screen** depending on whether you're using **gesture navigation** or the **Navigation Bar**.

1. **Using the Home Button**:

   - If your phone is set to use the **Navigation Bar** (with the buttons at the bottom), you can simply tap the **Home Button**. The **Home Button** is usually in the center of the navigation bar, and it looks like a small circle. When you tap it, you will immediately go back to the **Home Screen**.

2. **Using Gestures**:

   - If your phone is set to use **gesture navigation**, you won't see the buttons at the bottom. Instead, you'll use **gestures** to navigate.
   - To return to the **Home Screen** while using gestures, **swipe up** from the bottom of the screen. Start from the very bottom edge of the phone and swipe upward in a smooth motion. When you do this, you will return to the **Home Screen**.

Accessing Additional Home Screens

Your **Google Pixel 9 Pro** has multiple **Home Screens** that you can customize. Each screen can hold a different set of apps or widgets.

1. **Swipe Left or Right**:

   o To move between the **Home Screens**, you can simply swipe left or right on the **Home Screen**. This allows you to access additional screens where you can organize more apps or add different widgets.

2. **Switching Screens**:

   o You can keep swiping left or right until you reach the last **Home Screen**. Each screen is connected, so you can move through them seamlessly.

3. **Setting Up Multiple Home Screens**:

   o You can add more screens or remove ones that you don't use. To do this, tap and hold an empty space on your **Home Screen**, and then tap on **Home Settings** to add or remove screens.

Customizing the Home Screen

One of the great things about the **Google Pixel 9 Pro** is that you can customize your **Home Screen** to fit your preferences. You can organize your apps, change the wallpaper, and even add widgets. Let's go through each customization option in detail.

Adding Apps to the Home Screen

You can add any app to your **Home Screen** to make it easier to access. By placing apps on the **Home Screen**, you don't have to search through the **App Drawer** every time you want to use them. Here's how to do it:

1. **Open the App Drawer**:

    ○ To add an app to the **Home Screen**, you first need to open the **App Drawer**. The **App Drawer** is where all your apps are located. To open it, **swipe up** from the bottom of the screen.

2. **Find the App**:

    ○ Scroll through the list of apps or use the search bar at the top of the **App Drawer** to find the app you want to add to the **Home Screen**.

3. **Tap and Hold the App**:

    ○ Once you find the app, tap and hold on its icon. After a moment, a menu will appear with options like **Add to Home Screen** or **Remove from Home Screen**.

4. **Drag the App to the Home Screen**:

   - After tapping and holding the app, drag it to your **Home Screen**. You can place it anywhere you want on the screen.
   - When you release the app, it will be added to the **Home Screen**.

Organizing Apps on the Home Screen

Once you have multiple apps on your **Home Screen**, it's a good idea to organize them so you can easily find what you're looking for. You can create **folders** to group related apps together, like putting all your social media apps in one folder or all your shopping apps in another. Here's how to organize your apps:

1. **Create a Folder**:

   - Tap and hold one app icon that you want to place in a folder.
   - Then, drag that app over another app that you want to group it with. When the two apps overlap, you'll see the option to **create a folder**.

2. **Name the Folder**:

   - Once the folder is created, the phone will automatically assign a name to the folder, like **Social** or **Productivity**. You can change the name by tapping on the folder, then tapping on the **folder name** at the top and typing in a new name.

3. **Add More Apps to the Folder**:

   o   To add more apps to the folder, tap and hold an app icon, then drag it into the folder you created. Release the app to place it inside the folder.

4. **Remove Apps from a Folder**:

   o   If you want to remove an app from a folder, open the folder and tap and hold the app icon. Then drag it out of the folder and place it back on the **Home Screen**.

5. **Delete a Folder**:

   o   To delete a folder, simply drag all the apps out of the folder, leaving it empty. Once the folder is empty, it will automatically disappear from your **Home Screen**.

Setting Wallpapers on the Home Screen

Your **Home Screen** wallpaper is the background image that appears behind your apps. Changing the wallpaper allows you to personalize your phone and make it feel more like yours. Here's how to change the wallpaper on your **Google Pixel 9 Pro**:

1. **Tap and Hold on the Home Screen**:

   - Start by tapping and holding on an empty space on your **Home Screen**. This will bring up the **Home Screen settings**.

2. **Select Wallpapers**:

   - After holding on the Home Screen, a menu will appear at the bottom of the screen. Tap on **Wallpapers** to choose a new image.

3. **Choose a Wallpaper**:

   - You will see several options for **wallpapers**. You can choose from:
     - **Pre-installed Wallpapers**: These are wallpapers that come with your phone.
     - **Google Wallpapers**: These are beautiful and high-quality wallpapers that you can download from Google.
     - **Your Photos**: If you have photos on your phone, you can set one of your pictures as the wallpaper.

4. **Set the Wallpaper**:

- Once you've chosen your preferred wallpaper, tap **Set Wallpaper**. You will be asked if you want to apply the wallpaper to your **Home Screen**, **Lock Screen**, or both.
- Choose **Home Screen** (or both if you want the same wallpaper for the Lock Screen too) and tap **Set**.

Additional Customizations for the Home Screen

Now that you've learned how to add apps, organize them into folders, and change your wallpaper, let's explore a few other ways to personalize your **Home Screen**.

Adding Widgets

Widgets are small apps that show useful information right on your **Home Screen**. They can show things like the weather, your calendar, your to-do list, or even news updates. Here's how to add a widget:

1. **Tap and Hold on the Home Screen**:

   - Start by tapping and holding on an empty space on the **Home Screen**.

2. **Select Widgets**:

    ○ From the menu that appears, tap on
       Widgets. You will see a list of all
       available widgets.
3. **Choose a Widget**:

    ○ Scroll through the widgets and choose
       one you want to add, such as the
       Weather Widget, **Clock Widget**, or
       Google Search Widget.
4. **Drag the Widget to the Home Screen**:

    ○ Tap and hold the widget, then drag it to
       your **Home Screen**. Release it in the spot
       where you want it to appear.
5. **Resize the Widget**:

    ○ Some widgets can be resized. To resize a
       widget, tap and hold on it, then drag the
       edges to make it bigger or smaller.

Adjusting Icon Size and Layout

You can adjust the layout of the **Home Screen** to make
icons smaller or bigger. This will allow you to fit more
apps on the screen if you prefer.

1. **Go to Settings**:

- Open the **Settings** app and tap on **Display**.
2. **Select Home Screen**:

- Scroll down and tap on **Home Screen**.
3. **Adjust Icon Size**:

- You will see an option for **Icon Size**. You can adjust the slider to make icons bigger or smaller. This will change the size of the app icons on your **Home Screen**.
4. **Change Grid Layout**:

- You can also change the **grid layout** of the **Home Screen**, which determines how many icons can fit in each row and column. You can choose a **4x4 grid**, **5x5 grid**, or other options.

Conclusion

Customizing your **Google Pixel 9 Pro**'s **Home Screen** is an important way to make your phone feel personal and easy to use. In this chapter, we've covered how to navigate the **Home Screen**, add and organize apps, set wallpapers, and customize other aspects of the screen.

By following these simple steps, you can create a **Home Screen** that suits your needs and makes your phone more enjoyable to use. Whether you want a clean and simple layout or a vibrant, information-packed screen, the choice is yours.

In the next chapters, we will explore more features of your **Google Pixel 9 Pro**, such as the camera system, performance, and security options. Let's continue to explore your new device.

Using the App Drawer

The **App Drawer** is a place where all the apps you have installed on your **Google Pixel 9 Pro** are stored. It is like a big folder that keeps all your apps organized, so you can easily find and open any app whenever you need it.

Let's walk through how to use the **App Drawer** on your **Pixel 9 Pro**.

How to Open the App Drawer

1. **Swipe Up from the Bottom of the Screen**:
   - To open the **App Drawer**, all you need to do is swipe up from the very bottom edge of the screen. This means you should start your swipe from the very bottom of your phone and move your finger upward, toward the center of the screen.

- As you swipe up, you will see all the apps you have installed appear in a grid. This is the **App Drawer**.
- Once the **App Drawer** opens, you can scroll through it to find the app you want to use.

How to Find an App in the App Drawer

The **App Drawer** can get crowded as you install more apps, but don't worry! There are a couple of ways to find the app you need quickly.

1. **Scroll Through the App Drawer**:

   - To look through the apps, simply swipe up or down. The apps are listed alphabetically, so if you remember the name of the app you want, just scroll until you find it.
   - You can also swipe sideways to move through different pages of the **App Drawer**. Each page holds a set of apps, and you can keep swiping left or right until you find the app you're looking for.

2. **Use the Search Bar**:

   - At the top of the **App Drawer**, you will see a **search bar**. This search bar allows you to quickly find any app on your phone by typing the name of the app.

- To use the search bar, tap on it and type the name of the app you want to open. For example, if you're looking for the **YouTube** app, just type "YouTube" in the search bar. The app will appear in the search results below.
- This is a very fast way to find apps, especially when you have a lot of them installed.

How to Open an App

Once you've found the app you want to open, it's easy to launch it:

1. **Tap the App Icon**:

   - Simply tap on the app's icon, and the app will open. It will appear on your **Home Screen** or, if it's not there, it will take you to the app itself.

2. **Returning to the App Drawer**:

   - If you're using the app and want to go back to the **App Drawer**, you can press the **Home Button** (or swipe up if using gestures), and the **App Drawer** will be right there.

How to Organize Apps in the App Drawer

You can keep the **App Drawer** organized by creating folders. This way, apps that are related to each other can be grouped together, which helps keep everything neat.

1. **Create a Folder**:

   - To create a folder, tap and hold one app in the **App Drawer**. Then, drag it over another app that you want to group it with. When the apps overlap, a folder will be created automatically.

2. **Name the Folder**:

   - After creating the folder, you can give it a name. For example, you could name a folder "Social" for all your social media apps like Facebook, Instagram, and Twitter. To name a folder, open it and tap the **folder name** at the top to edit it.

3. **Add More Apps to the Folder**:

   - To add more apps to a folder, tap and hold any other app and drag it into the folder. Release it inside the folder, and it will be grouped with the other apps.

4. **Remove an App from a Folder**:

   - If you want to remove an app from a folder, open the folder and tap and hold the app. Then, drag it out of the folder

and release it on the **Home Screen** or in
the **App Drawer**.

How to Remove Apps from the App Drawer

Sometimes, you may want to remove apps from the **App
Drawer** to keep things tidy. However, you can't delete
apps directly from the **App Drawer**. You will need to go
into the **Settings** to uninstall an app.

1. **Go to Settings**:

   ○ Open the **Settings** app and tap **Apps &
     Notifications**.
2. **Select the App You Want to Uninstall**:

   ○ From the list of apps, find the one you
     want to remove and tap on it. Then, tap
     Uninstall and confirm that you want to
     remove it from your phone.

Adjusting Refresh Rate

The **refresh rate** of your phone's display determines
how smooth the screen looks when you scroll or interact
with it. A higher refresh rate, like **120Hz**, makes
everything look smoother when you swipe or scroll
through apps. This can improve your experience by
making the phone feel faster and more responsive.

By default, the **Pixel 9 Pro** is set to **120Hz** for smooth scrolling. However, if you want to change this setting or if you want to save some battery life, you can adjust the refresh rate.

Let's explore how to adjust the **refresh rate** on your **Google Pixel 9 Pro**.

How to Adjust the Refresh Rate

1. **Go to Settings**:

   ○ To begin, open the **Settings** app from the **Home Screen** or **App Drawer**.

2. **Select Display**:

   ○ Scroll down and tap on **Display**. This will open the display settings, where you can adjust different options for your screen.

3. **Tap on Smooth Display**:

   ○ Under the **Display** settings, find the option called **Smooth Display**. Tap on it to open the settings for the refresh rate.

4. **Toggle Between 60Hz and 120Hz**:

   ○ You will now see two options for the refresh rate: **60Hz** and **120Hz**.

     ■ **120Hz** is the default setting, and it provides smoother scrolling and a

more fluid experience when using apps.
- **60Hz** is the lower setting, and it can help save battery life by reducing the refresh rate.
  - To choose **120Hz**, just make sure the toggle is on. If you want to switch to **60Hz**, turn off the toggle for **120Hz**.

Why Choose 120Hz or 60Hz?

- **120Hz**:

  - The **120Hz refresh rate** makes everything on your phone's display feel smoother. Scrolling through social media, browsing websites, and navigating through apps will feel more fluid and faster.
  - However, the **120Hz refresh rate** uses more battery power because it refreshes the screen faster, so if you want the smoothest experience and don't mind using more battery, keep it on **120Hz**.
- **60Hz**:

  - The **60Hz refresh rate** is a standard refresh rate for many smartphones. While it's not as smooth as **120Hz**, it uses less

power, which can help save your phone's
battery.
- If you are trying to extend battery life and
  don't mind a slightly less smooth
  experience, **60Hz** is a good option.

When to Use 60Hz or 120Hz

1. **For Better Battery Life**:

   - If you are using your phone for long
     periods of time or want to save battery,
     switching to **60Hz** might be helpful. It will
     reduce power consumption and extend
     the battery life of your **Pixel 9 Pro**.
2. **For Smoother Scrolling**:

   - If you use your phone for tasks like
     gaming, watching videos, or just prefer
     smoother scrolling and animations,
     120Hz is the way to go. This refresh rate
     is especially noticeable in apps that
     involve a lot of movement, like **YouTube**,
     Instagram, or **Twitter**.
3. **Switching Back and Forth**:

   - If you want to use **120Hz** for smoother
     performance during high-demand tasks
     but conserve battery at other times, feel
     free to switch back and forth. You can

easily toggle between **60Hz** and **120Hz** at any time in the settings.

Conclusion

In this chapter, we have learned how to navigate the **App Drawer** and how to adjust the **refresh rate** for your **Google Pixel 9 Pro**. We covered how to open the **App Drawer**, find apps, create folders, and organize everything for easy access. We also discussed how to adjust the **refresh rate** to either **60Hz** or **120Hz** based on your preferences for smoothness or battery life.

Now that you understand how to navigate and customize your **Home Screen** and display settings, you can make your phone work better for you. Whether you want to keep your apps organized, choose a smoother display experience, or conserve battery life, these settings will help you get the most out of your **Google Pixel 9 Pro**.

In the next chapters, we will dive into other important features, including the **camera system, security settings**, and more. Let's keep exploring!

Chapter Three

Mastering the Camera System

The **Google Pixel 9 Pro** has one of the best camera systems available on any smartphone. It's known for capturing stunning photos and videos, whether you're in bright sunlight or a low-light environment. The phone comes with advanced camera features like **Portrait Mode**, **Night Sight**, and **Super Res Zoom**, which can help you take professional-looking pictures. In this chapter, we'll dive into how to use these features to get the best results from your camera.

Accessing the Camera App

The first step to taking photos and videos on your **Google Pixel 9 Pro** is to open the **Camera app**. The camera is easy to access and simple to use. Here's how you can open the Camera app and start taking great pictures:

Method 1: Open the Camera from the Home Screen

1. **Locate the Camera App Icon:**

   - On your **Home Screen**, you should see the **Camera app** icon. It looks like a small camera lens. Tap on the icon to open the app.

2. **Tap the Camera Icon**:

   ○ After you tap the icon, the camera will open, and you'll see the camera interface where you can begin taking photos and videos.

Method 2: Use the Volume Down Button to Open the Camera

1. **Press the Volume Down Button Twice**:

   ○ If you prefer to quickly open the camera, you can press the **Volume Down** button twice. This feature can be turned on or off in the settings. It's a fast shortcut to get to the camera whenever you need it, especially if you're in a hurry to snap a photo.

2. **Camera Interface**:

   ○ Once the camera is open, you'll see a live preview of what the camera is pointing at. You can adjust the settings and select different lenses from the options at the top of the screen.

Selecting Between Lenses

The **Google Pixel 9 Pro** comes with three camera lenses: **Wide**, **Ultra-wide**, and **Telephoto**. These lenses give you different perspectives and allow you to take various types of photos.

Wide Lens (Standard Camera)

- The **Wide lens** is the main camera lens. It's the one you will use most often for everyday photos. The lens captures a **standard field of view** and is perfect for most situations like portraits, landscapes, and everyday snapshots.

Ultra-wide Lens

- The **Ultra-wide lens** allows you to capture a much **wider view** than the **Wide lens**. This is useful when you want to take pictures of big groups of people, large landscapes, or even tall buildings. It captures a wider scene in one shot, making it perfect for capturing more of your surroundings.

Telephoto Lens

- The **Telephoto lens** is designed to **zoom in** on distant objects without losing image quality. You can use the **Telephoto lens** when you want to capture details from far away, like wildlife or distant landmarks. This lens allows for up to **5x**

optical zoom, which is much clearer than digital zoom.

To switch between the lenses, you simply tap the options at the top of the camera interface. You'll see **Wide**, **Ultra-wide**, and **Telephoto** icons. Tap on the one you want to use, and the camera will automatically switch.

Taking Photos with the Google Pixel 9 Pro

The **Google Pixel 9 Pro** makes it easy to take beautiful photos, thanks to its powerful camera system. In this section, we'll go through some of the most popular modes and features that can help you take amazing pictures.

Portrait Mode

Portrait Mode is a feature that helps you take professional-looking photos where the background is blurred, and the subject stands out sharply. This is called a **bokeh effect**, and it makes your subject look sharp and clear while creating a beautiful, blurry background.

Here's how to use **Portrait Mode**:

1. **Open the Camera App:**

- Start by opening the **Camera app**.
2. **Select Portrait Mode**:

    - At the top of the screen, you will see a selection of modes. One of the options will be **Portrait**. Tap on it to enable **Portrait Mode**.
3. **Position Your Subject**:

    - Once you're in **Portrait Mode**, position the subject of your photo (like a person, pet, or object) within the frame. The camera will automatically detect the subject and blur the background for a professional look.
4. **Take the Picture**:

    - Press the **shutter button** to take the photo. The camera will apply the **bokeh effect**, making the subject look sharp and the background beautifully blurred.

Night Sight

The **Night Sight** feature is one of the most powerful tools on the **Google Pixel 9 Pro**. It allows you to take clear, bright pictures even in **low light**. If you've ever tried to take a photo in a dimly lit room or at night and it came out too dark, **Night Sight** can help.

Here's how to use **Night Sight**:

1. **Open the Camera App**:

   - Open the **Camera app**.

2. **Switch to Night Sight**:

   - If the lighting is low, the camera will automatically suggest **Night Sight**. Alternatively, you can tap the **Night Sight** mode at the top of the screen.

3. **Hold Steady and Capture the Image**:

   - Hold your phone steady as the camera takes the picture. The **Pixel 9 Pro** uses its AI technology to brighten the image and reduce noise, so you'll get a much clearer picture than with a regular camera mode.

4. **Adjust Exposure (If Needed)**:

   - You may see a **slider** for exposure at the bottom of the screen. If the image looks too dark or too light, you can adjust the exposure by sliding it left or right.

5. **Take the Picture**:

   - Once you've set up your shot and adjusted the exposure (if needed), press the **shutter button**. The camera will use **Night Sight** to capture a bright, detailed photo even in low light.

Super Res Zoom

The **Super Res Zoom** feature allows you to zoom in on objects or subjects that are far away. The **Pixel 9 Pro** uses AI to **sharpen** the zoomed-in image and reduce any blurriness that might happen when zooming in digitally.

Here's how to use **Super Res Zoom**:

1. **Open the Camera App:**

   ○ Open the **Camera app**.
2. **Zoom In on Your Subject:**

   ○ To use **Super Res Zoom**, tap and hold the **zoom slider** on the camera interface. You will see options like **1x**, **2x**, **5x**, and so on. Slide it to zoom in on the object or person you want to capture.
3. **Use the Zoom Slider for Clarity:**

   ○ As you zoom in, the **Pixel 9 Pro** will use its **AI technology** to enhance the image. The more you zoom in, the clearer the image will be, even if you're zooming in on a far-away subject.
4. **Take the Picture:**

   ○ Once you have zoomed in and positioned your subject, press the **shutter button** to

take the photo. You should see a sharp
and clear image, even if the subject is far
away.

Using the Camera for Videos

The **Google Pixel 9 Pro** is not just for photos; you can
also record videos in high quality.

1. **Switch to Video Mode**:

   ○ To start recording a video, open the
   Camera app, then swipe to **Video Mode**.
   You will see a small **video camera icon**
   at the bottom of the screen.

2. **Record the Video**:

   ○ Tap the **record button** to start filming.
   The **Pixel 9 Pro** records in high-quality
   4K and **1080p** resolution, giving you
   detailed and sharp videos.

3. **Zoom While Recording**:

   ○ While recording a video, you can use the
   zoom slider to zoom in or out on the
   subject. The camera will adjust the zoom
   without affecting the video's quality.

4. **Stop Recording**:

- To stop the video, press the **stop button**. The video will automatically save in your **Gallery**.

Tips for Better Photos and Videos

1. **Lighting is Key**:

   - Always try to take photos in well-lit areas. Good lighting can make a huge difference in the quality of your photos. If you're indoors, consider using natural light from windows or adding more light sources.

2. **Use the Grid Lines**:

   - The **Pixel 9 Pro** offers grid lines that can help you align your photos. You can turn this feature on in the camera settings. Grid lines help you apply the **rule of thirds** for more balanced compositions.

3. **Don't Shake the Camera**:

   - When taking photos or videos, keep your hands steady. Even the smallest shake can make your photos blurry. Use both hands to hold the phone steady or rest your elbows on a solid surface.

4. **Explore Pro Mode (Optional)**:

- If you want more control over your photos, you can explore **Pro Mode** in the camera settings. This mode lets you adjust things like **ISO**, **shutter speed**, and **white balance** for more professional-looking photos.

Conclusion

The **Google Pixel 9 Pro** camera system is designed to help you take the best photos and videos in any situation. From the **Portrait Mode** for professional-looking shots to the **Night Sight** for low-light conditions, this phone's camera is powerful and easy to use. Whether you're capturing memories with friends, snapping a picture of nature, or zooming in on distant objects, the **Pixel 9 Pro** can help you get stunning results.

Now that you understand how to use the camera, it's time to start experimenting and taking pictures. With practice, you'll learn how to use all the features to their fullest potential and capture beautiful moments with ease.

In the next chapters, we will explore more features of your **Google Pixel 9 Pro**, including how to optimize its performance, customize settings, and make the most of its other tools.

Camera Settings and Recording Videos on the Google Pixel 9 Pro

In this chapter, we will walk you through the various **camera settings** of your **Google Pixel 9 Pro**, including how to adjust photo resolution, use the **HDR+** feature, and set up the **Flash**. We will also cover how to record high-quality **videos** with options like **4K recording**, **optical zoom**, and **stabilization** for smooth shots.

Your **Pixel 9 Pro** has an advanced camera system that allows you to control many aspects of your photos and videos. We'll guide you through all of these settings in a simple, step-by-step manner to help you make the most of your phone's camera.

Camera Settings: How to Adjust Your Camera for the Best Photos

The **camera settings** on your **Google Pixel 9 Pro** allow you to customize the way your photos look and work. Whether you want higher resolution, better lighting, or specific photo effects, the settings are all there to make your experience better.

Accessing the Camera Settings

1. **Open the Camera App:**

- Start by opening the **Camera app** on your **Google Pixel 9 Pro**. You can either tap on the Camera icon from the **Home Screen** or use the **Volume Down** button shortcut, as explained earlier in this guide.

2. **Find the Gear Icon**:

- Once the camera interface is open, you will see several icons at the top of the screen. Tap on the **gear icon** (this represents **Settings**) to open the **Camera Settings** menu.

Photo Resolution

One of the most important settings for your photos is the **photo resolution**. This controls how detailed your photos are. The higher the resolution, the more detail your photos will have, which is great for printing or cropping.

The **Google Pixel 9 Pro** offers two main photo resolutions: **12.2 MP** (Standard) and **50 MP** (Higher Detail). Here's how to choose the right resolution for your photos:

1. **Set the Photo Resolution**:

- In the **Camera Settings** menu, scroll down until you see the **Photo Resolution** option.
- By default, the camera is set to **12.2 MP**, which provides excellent quality for most uses. If you want more detail, you can switch to **50 MP** resolution, which captures higher detail for larger prints or heavy cropping.

2. **How to Select 12.2 MP or 50 MP**:

- Tap on the **Photo Resolution** option, and a menu will pop up with two choices:
  - **12.2 MP**: The standard resolution for regular photos.
  - **50 MP**: The high-resolution option for greater detail.
- Choose **12.2 MP** for everyday photos or **50 MP** for photos that require extra sharpness and clarity.

3. **When to Use 50 MP**:

- The **50 MP** resolution is ideal when you want the highest quality photo, especially in situations where you want to crop the photo later or make large prints. Keep in mind that **50 MP photos** can take up more storage space on your phone.

4. **When to Use 12.2 MP**:

- The **12.2 MP** setting is perfect for most photos, including portraits, landscapes, and snapshots. It provides a good balance of quality and file size, so you can take many photos without filling up your storage too quickly.

Using HDR+

The **HDR+** (High Dynamic Range) feature is a powerful tool that helps you take better photos in challenging lighting conditions. When you're shooting in environments where there's a strong contrast between light and dark areas—such as in bright sunlight or when taking photos indoors—it can be hard to get a good shot. **HDR+** helps by balancing the lighting in your photos, making dark areas brighter and bright areas more detailed.

Here's how to turn on **HDR+**:

1. **Enable HDR+**:

   - In the **Camera Settings**, scroll down until you find the **HDR+** option.
   - Tap on the toggle to turn **HDR+** on or off. The camera will automatically use **HDR+** in situations where it will improve your photo quality.

2. **When to Use HDR+:**

   - **HDR+** is great for photos taken in high-contrast scenes, like when you're taking pictures outside in the sun or inside with a bright window in the background. It helps bring out the details in shadows and highlights.
   - If you are taking a photo of a sunset, for example, **HDR+** will ensure that the sky looks vibrant while still showing details in the shadows, like the landscape or people in the foreground.

Using the Flash

The **flash** can be used to light up a scene when you're taking a photo in low-light conditions. The **Pixel 9 Pro** offers a **flash** option that can be turned on, off, or set to automatic.

Here's how to adjust the **flash** settings:

1. **Turn the Flash On or Off:**

   - In the camera interface, you'll see a small **flash icon** (it looks like a lightning bolt) at the top of the screen.
   - Tap the **flash icon** to toggle between three options:

- **Off**: The flash will not be used.
- **Auto**: The camera will decide when to use the flash (usually in low light).
- **On**: The flash will be used every time you take a photo, even in bright light.

2. **When to Use the Flash**:

   - Use the **flash** when you're taking pictures in **low-light** environments. It will help illuminate the scene and make your photo clearer.
   - If you're outside in **bright daylight**, it's usually better to leave the flash off, as it can create unwanted shadows or reflections.

Recording Videos with the Google Pixel 9 Pro

The **Google Pixel 9 Pro** doesn't just take amazing photos—it also lets you record high-quality videos. The phone can record videos in **4K**, giving you excellent video quality. You can also use the **5x optical zoom** while recording videos and activate **stabilization** for smoother footage.

Let's explore how to record videos and adjust video settings on your **Pixel 9 Pro**.

How to Record Videos

1. **Open the Camera App**:

   - Start by opening the **Camera app**. If you are in photo mode, you can swipe the screen or tap the **video camera icon** to switch to **Video Mode**.

2. **Tap the Video Camera Icon**:

   - In the camera interface, you'll see a **video camera icon** at the bottom of the screen. Tap this icon to switch the camera to video recording mode.

3. **Start Recording**:

   - To begin recording, simply press the **red record button**. The phone will start capturing video immediately. You'll see a **timer** counting up, indicating the length of the video.

4. **Zoom While Recording**:

   - While recording, you can **zoom in** by using the **zoom slider** on the screen. You can zoom in up to **5x** using the **optical**

zoom, which gives you clear and sharp video even at a distance.

5. **Stop Recording:**

   ○ When you're ready to stop recording, press the **stop button** (the red square) to end the video. The video will automatically be saved to your **Gallery** for easy access.

Recording 4K Videos

The **Google Pixel 9 Pro** can record videos in **4K**, which provides stunning video quality, with clearer details and better color accuracy. If you want to record a video in **4K**, here's how you can change the video resolution settings:

1. **Go to Video Settings:**

   ○ While in **Video Mode**, tap the **Settings icon** (gear icon) at the top of the camera interface.

2. **Select Video Resolution:**

   ○ In the video settings, look for the **Video Resolution** option. Tap on it to choose your preferred resolution.

3. **Select 4K Resolution**:

   ○ You will see different resolution options, such as **1080p** and **4K**. Tap on **4K** to enable **4K recording** at either **30 FPS** or **60 FPS**. Higher **frame rates** (FPS) result in smoother videos, so choose **60 FPS** if you want super-smooth footage.

Using Optical Zoom and Stabilization

When recording videos, the **Google Pixel 9 Pro** allows you to zoom in up to **5x** without losing image quality, thanks to its **optical zoom** feature. Additionally, you can activate **video stabilization** to reduce shakiness in your videos and make them smoother.

1. **Use Optical Zoom While Recording**:

   ○ While recording, use the **zoom slider** to zoom in on distant objects. The **Pixel 9 Pro** uses **5x optical zoom**, which maintains the video quality without making the image blurry or pixelated.

2. **Turn on Stabilization**:

   ○ To turn on **video stabilization**, go to the **Camera Settings** and scroll down to the **Stabilization** option. Make sure it is toggled on. Stabilization helps reduce the shaky movements when filming, especially when you're walking or holding the camera with one hand.

Conclusion

The **Google Pixel 9 Pro** is a powerhouse when it comes to photography and video recording. With its **HDR+** feature, **Night Sight**, and **Super Res Zoom**, you can take amazing photos in any lighting condition. The camera settings, like adjusting **photo resolution** and using the **flash**, allow you to tailor the experience to your needs. For videos, you can shoot in **4K**, zoom in with **5x optical zoom**, and use **stabilization** for smooth footage.

By following the steps in this chapter, you now have a solid understanding of how to master your **Pixel 9 Pro** camera. Whether you're taking stunning photos or recording high-quality videos, your **Pixel 9 Pro** camera has all the features you need to capture beautiful moments.

Let's continue exploring other features of your **Google Pixel 9 Pro** in the following chapters!

Chapter Four

Optimizing Performance of Your Google Pixel 9 Pro

In this chapter, we will show you how to make sure your **Google Pixel 9 Pro** runs smoothly. Over time, as you use your phone, apps, photos, and other files can take up space and slow down the phone. By following a few simple steps, you can improve the performance of your phone and make sure it works as fast as when you first got it. We'll also cover how to manage storage and free up space, which will help your phone run better.

Managing Storage

One of the most important things to keep in mind for optimal performance is **storage**. If your phone is full of apps, photos, videos, and other data, it can start to slow down. But don't worry! We will explain how to check your available storage and clear up space so your **Google Pixel 9 Pro** continues to perform at its best.

How to Check Available Storage on Your Pixel 9 Pro

Checking your available storage is the first step in understanding what is taking up space on your phone. Once you know what's using up your storage, you can make smart decisions about what to delete or move to free up space.

1. **Open the Settings App**:

   o To begin, open the **Settings** app on your **Google Pixel 9 Pro**. You can find the **Settings** app on your **Home Screen** or in the **App Drawer**.

2. **Tap on Storage**:

   o Scroll down and tap on **Storage**. This section of the **Settings** will give you an overview of how much space is being used and how much is available.

3. **View Storage Usage**:

   o In the **Storage** section, you will see a breakdown of what is using your storage. This includes things like:
      - **Apps**: All the apps you have installed.
      - **Photos & Videos**: Your photos and videos.
      - **Music & Audio**: Music files or other audio files.
      - **Downloads**: Files you have downloaded.
   o It will also show you how much space is **free** and how much is **used**.

What to Do When You're Running Low on Storage

When your phone is getting close to being full, it's time to make some decisions about what to keep and what to delete. Here are a few ways to free up space on your **Pixel 9 Pro**.

Delete Unused Apps or Large Files

Over time, you might have installed apps you no longer use or downloaded large files like videos or music that take up a lot of space. Here's how to find and remove those files:

Step 1: Uninstall Unused Apps

1. **Go to Settings:**

   - Open the **Settings** app on your phone.
2. **Tap on Apps & Notifications:**

   - Scroll down and select **Apps & Notifications** to see all the apps installed on your phone.
3. **Select the App You Want to Uninstall:**

   - Tap on **See All Apps** to see the full list of apps. Scroll through the list to find apps that you no longer need.

4. **Uninstall the App**:

   - Once you select the app, tap on it and you will see the option to **Uninstall**. Tap **Uninstall** to remove the app from your phone.

5. **Confirm the Uninstallation**:

   - A pop-up will ask if you're sure you want to uninstall the app. Tap **OK** or **Uninstall** to confirm.

Removing apps you don't use will immediately free up space and help your phone run faster.

Step 2: Delete Large Files (Videos, Music, and Downloads)

1. **Open the File Manager**:

   - Your **Google Pixel 9 Pro** has a **File Manager** that helps you find large files, like videos, music, and documents. Open the **Files** app on your phone. You can find this in the **App Drawer**.

2. **Check for Large Files**:

   - In the **Files** app, you'll see a section for **Storage**. Tap on it to see what files are taking up space. You can sort them by size to find the biggest files.

3. **Delete Unnecessary Files**:

   ○ If you see videos, music, or other files
     you don't need, you can delete them. Tap
     and hold on the file, then tap **Delete** or
     the trash can icon.

Deleting unnecessary files will make space for new
photos, apps, and updates while also helping the phone
run more efficiently.

Use Google Photos to Backup Your Photos and Videos

One of the easiest ways to save space on your **Google
Pixel 9 Pro** is by using **Google Photos** to **back up** your
photos and videos to the cloud. Once your photos and
videos are safely backed up, you can delete them from
your phone without losing them.

Step 1: Download Google Photos

1. **Install Google Photos**:

   ○ If you don't already have **Google Photos**
     installed on your phone, open the **Google
     Play Store** and search for **Google
     Photos**. Tap **Install** to download the app.

2. **Sign In to Your Google Account**:

   ○ Open the **Google Photos** app and sign in with your **Google Account**.

Step 2: Back Up Your Photos and Videos

1. **Enable Backup**:

   ○ Once you're signed in, open the **Google Photos** app. Tap on the **menu icon** (three horizontal lines) in the top left corner, and go to **Settings**.

2. **Turn On Backup & Sync**:

   ○ In **Settings**, find **Backup & Sync** and make sure it's turned on. This will automatically back up all your photos and videos to **Google Drive**.

3. **Choose Your Backup Settings**:

   ○ You can choose the quality of the backup. You can select **High Quality** for free unlimited storage, or **Original Quality** for full-resolution photos and videos (which will count against your **Google Drive** storage).

4. **Wait for the Backup to Complete**:

   ○ After turning on **Backup & Sync**, Google Photos will start uploading your photos and videos to the cloud. You'll be able to see the progress in the app.

Step 3: Delete Photos and Videos from Your Phone

1. **Delete Photos**:

   - Once your photos and videos are backed up, you can free up space on your phone by deleting them. In the **Google Photos** app, you'll see a **Free Up Space** option in **Settings**. Tap it, and Google Photos will automatically remove the photos and videos that have already been backed up to the cloud.

2. **Keep Your Photos Safe**:

   - Even though you delete photos from your phone, they are still saved in **Google Photos** in the cloud. You can access them anytime by opening the **Google Photos** app or visiting the **Google Photos** website.

Use Google Drive to Backup Documents and Files

Just like with photos and videos, you can use **Google Drive** to back up your documents and other important files, ensuring they're safe and freeing up space on your phone.

1. **Upload Files to Google Drive**:

   - Open the **Google Drive** app on your **Pixel 9 Pro**. If you don't have it installed, download it from the **Google Play Store**.
   - Tap the **plus (+) icon** and select **Upload**. Choose the files you want to upload from your phone's storage.

2. **Access Your Files from Any Device**:

   - Once your files are uploaded to **Google Drive**, you can access them from any device by signing into your **Google Account** and visiting **drive.google.com**.

By uploading documents and files to **Google Drive**, you can keep them safe and free up space on your phone.

Managing App Data and Cache

Sometimes apps store unnecessary data or **cache** files, which can take up storage space. You can manage this data to keep your phone running smoothly.

1. **Clear App Cache**:

- To clear the cache for a specific app, go to **Settings > Apps & Notifications > See All Apps**.
- Find and select the app you want to clear the cache for. Then, tap **Storage & Cache**, and tap **Clear Cache**. This will remove temporary files that might be taking up space.

2. **Clear App Data**:

- If you need to free up even more space, you can clear **app data**. This will delete everything stored in the app, including preferences and settings, so use it carefully.
- To clear **app data**, go to **Settings > Apps & Notifications > See All Apps**, select the app, tap **Storage & Cache**, and then tap **Clear Storage** or **Clear Data**.

Check Storage Usage Regularly

It's a good idea to check your storage usage regularly, so you can stay on top of how much space is being used. Here's how to do that:

1. **Go to Settings**:

- Open the **Settings** app.
2. **Tap on Storage**:

   - Scroll down and tap **Storage** to see an overview of how much space is being used.
3. **Manage Space**:

   - In this section, you can see which apps and files are taking up the most space. From here, you can decide if you want to delete anything, move files to the cloud, or uninstall apps.

Conclusion

Managing your **storage** is a key part of keeping your **Google Pixel 9 Pro** running smoothly. By following the steps in this chapter, you can easily free up space and ensure your phone continues to work at its best. Whether you delete unused apps, use **Google Photos** to back up your pictures, or upload documents to **Google Drive**, there are plenty of ways to manage storage on your phone.

In the next chapters, we will continue exploring other ways to optimize your **Google Pixel 9 Pro** and make the most of its features. By taking control of storage and performance, you'll ensure that your phone works quickly and efficiently for years to come.

Maximizing Battery Life and Boosting Performance on Your Google Pixel 9 Pro

In this chapter, we will focus on two important aspects of your **Google Pixel 9 Pro**: **maximizing battery life** and **boosting performance**. Over time, as you use your phone for different tasks, it can slow down or drain the battery faster. However, with a few simple settings and practices, you can keep your phone running longer without charging it and make sure it performs as fast as it did when you first got it.

Let's walk through easy-to-follow steps for both maximizing battery life and boosting performance.

Maximizing Battery Life

Battery life is one of the most important factors in how much you can enjoy your phone. A phone with a good battery life means you can use your phone throughout the day without needing to constantly charge it. Fortunately, your **Google Pixel 9 Pro** offers several features that help you manage and extend your battery life. Here are the main ways to save battery while using your phone.

Step 1: Enable Battery Saver

Battery Saver is a feature that reduces the power consumption of your phone. When you enable **Battery Saver**, your phone will limit background processes, reduce screen brightness, and disable certain non-essential features to help the battery last longer.

1. **Go to Settings**:

   - Open the **Settings** app from your **Home Screen** or **App Drawer**.
2. **Tap on Battery**:

   - Scroll down and tap on **Battery** in the **Settings** menu.
3. **Select Battery Saver**:

   - In the **Battery** section, you'll see an option called **Battery Saver**. Tap on it to open the settings.
4. **Turn on Battery Saver**:

   - To enable **Battery Saver**, toggle the switch to the **on** position. Once enabled, **Battery Saver** will automatically reduce power usage to help your phone last longer.
5. **When to Use Battery Saver**:

- ○ **Battery Saver** is perfect when your battery is running low, and you need your phone to last longer. It is especially useful during the day when you're out and about, and you don't have access to a charger.

Step 2: Set Up Adaptive Battery

Adaptive Battery is a smart feature that helps your phone manage battery usage. It learns which apps you use the most and prioritizes battery power for those apps. Apps you don't use often get limited background activity, which helps save battery life.

1. **Go to Settings**:

   - ○ Open the **Settings** app.
2. **Tap on Battery**:

   - ○ Scroll down and tap on **Battery**.
3. **Select Adaptive Battery**:

   - ○ In the **Battery** settings, tap on **Adaptive Battery**.
4. **Enable Adaptive Battery**:

   - ○ Toggle the switch to the **on** position. When **Adaptive Battery** is on, your phone will automatically adjust power usage based on your app activity and keep the battery usage efficient.

5. **How It Works**:

   ○ **Adaptive Battery** keeps track of the apps you use regularly, like **Gmail**, **YouTube**, or **WhatsApp**, and gives them more power. It limits background usage for apps you rarely use, so your phone doesn't waste battery on them.

Step 3: Use Extreme Battery Saver

If you need your phone to last as long as possible, even beyond **Battery Saver**, **Extreme Battery Saver** is your best option. This mode can help your **Google Pixel 9 Pro** last up to **72 hours** on a single charge by turning off most background processes and apps.

1. **Go to Settings**:

   ○ Open the **Settings** app.
2. **Tap on Battery**:

   ○ Scroll down and tap on **Battery**.
3. **Select Extreme Battery Saver**:

   ○ In the **Battery** menu, you'll find **Extreme Battery Saver**. Tap on it to open the feature.

4. **Enable Extreme Battery Saver**:

    ○ Tap **Turn On** to enable this mode. Once
      activated, your phone will turn off almost
      all non-essential apps and services. Only
      the most essential apps, like **Phone**,
      Messages, and **Clock**, will continue to
      run.

5. **When to Use Extreme Battery Saver**:

    ○ Use **Extreme Battery Saver** when you're
      in an emergency and need your phone to
      last as long as possible. It's perfect for
      long days where you might not have
      access to a charger, like during a long
      flight or road trip.

6. **How Extreme Battery Saver Works**:

    ○ **Extreme Battery Saver** reduces battery
      use by stopping most background
      activities. This helps your **Pixel 9 Pro** last
      for days on a single charge. However,
      keep in mind that this mode will limit your
      ability to use many apps until you turn it
      off.

Boosting Performance

While **battery life** is crucial, **performance** is just as important. A phone that runs slowly or is laggy can make using it frustrating. Fortunately, there are several settings and techniques you can use to make sure your **Google Pixel 9 Pro** continues to perform well and stay fast.

Step 1: Disable Unused Background Apps

Apps that run in the background can consume memory and processing power, slowing down your phone. Disabling or closing apps you're not using will help improve the performance of your **Google Pixel 9 Pro**.

1. **Go to Settings**:

   ○ Open the **Settings** app.
2. **Tap on Apps & Notifications**:

   ○ Scroll down and tap on **Apps & Notifications** to see the list of apps that are running.
3. **See All Apps**:

   ○ Tap on **See All Apps** to open the complete list of apps installed on your phone.
4. **Close Background Apps**:

   ○ Tap on any app that you're not using. If the app is running in the background, you'll see the option to **Force Stop** it. Tap on **Force Stop** to stop the app from using resources in the background.

5. **Use the Recent Apps Menu**:

    o   You can also close apps by swiping up from the bottom of the screen to open the **Recent Apps** menu. Swipe left or right to find the apps you want to close, then swipe them off the screen to remove them.

By regularly closing unused background apps, you can ensure that your phone has more memory and processing power available for the apps you're using.

Step 2: Turn Off Animations for a Faster Feel

While animations can make your phone look more interesting, they can also slow it down. By turning off some of the animations, you can make your phone feel faster.

1. **Enable Developer Options**:

    o   First, you need to enable **Developer Options**. To do this, go to **Settings > About Phone** and tap on **Build Number** seven times. This will unlock **Developer Options** in the **Settings**.

2. **Go to Developer Options**:

   ○ Now, go to **Settings > System > Developer Options**.
3. **Turn Off Window and Transition Animations**:

   ○ In **Developer Options**, you'll see options like **Window Animation Scale**, **Transition Animation Scale**, and **Animator Duration Scale**. Tap on each of these options and set them to **Off**. This will turn off most of the animations on your phone, making everything feel faster and more responsive.
4. **Optional**: If you don't want to completely turn off animations, you can set these options to a lower value (for example, change the scale from **1x** to **0.5x**) to make the animations faster without removing them completely.

Step 3: Regularly Clear Cache

Cached data is stored by apps to help them load faster. However, over time, this data can build up and take up storage space, which can slow down your phone. It's a good idea to clear the cache regularly to keep your phone running smoothly.

1. **Go to Settings**:

- Open the **Settings** app.
2. **Tap on Storage**:

    - Scroll down and tap on **Storage**.
3. **Select Cached Data**:

    - In the **Storage** section, you will see an option for **Cached Data**. Tap on it to see how much cached data is stored on your phone.
4. **Clear Cached Data**:

    - Tap **Clear Cached Data** to remove all cached data. Don't worry—this won't delete your app data, photos, or messages. It only removes temporary files that can safely be deleted.

By clearing cached data regularly, you can free up space and ensure that your phone remains fast and responsive.

Other Tips for Boosting Performance

- **Restart Your Phone**:

    - If your phone feels slow, a simple restart can help clear up memory and close unnecessary processes. To restart your

Google Pixel 9 Pro, press and hold the **power button** until the menu appears, then select **Restart**.

- **Update Apps and Software**:

    ○ Keeping your apps and software up to date is important for performance. To update apps, go to the **Google Play Store** and tap **Update All**. To update your phone's software, go to **Settings > System > Software Update**.

- **Factory Reset**:

    ○ If your phone is still sluggish after trying all these steps, you may want to consider performing a **factory reset**. This will erase all data from the phone and restore it to its original state, which can help fix any software issues. Before doing this, be sure to back up your data. To factory reset your **Pixel 9 Pro**, go to **Settings > System > Reset Options** and tap **Erase All Data**.

Conclusion

In this chapter, we've covered a range of ways to maximize the **battery life** and **performance** of your **Google Pixel 9 Pro**. By enabling **Battery Saver**, using

Adaptive Battery, and activating **Extreme Battery Saver**, you can extend your battery life for longer usage. On the performance side, we've shown you how to manage background apps, turn off animations, and clear cache to make your phone faster and more responsive.

By following these tips and making these adjustments, you'll ensure that your **Google Pixel 9 Pro** continues to run smoothly and efficiently for as long as possible.

System Updates on Your Google Pixel 9 Pro

In this chapter, we will explore the importance of keeping your **Google Pixel 9 Pro** up to date with the latest **system updates**. Updates are crucial for maintaining the performance, security, and functionality of your phone. They help fix bugs, improve features, and protect you from security threats. We will guide you through the process of checking for and installing **system updates** to make sure your phone is always running smoothly and securely.

What are System Updates?

System updates are software upgrades that are released by **Google** for your **Pixel 9 Pro**. These updates include:

1. **Security Patches**: Updates that fix any vulnerabilities that might let hackers or malware get into your phone.
2. **New Features**: Updates can introduce new functions or improve existing features. For example, a system update might add a new way to interact with the screen or improve the camera.
3. **Bug Fixes**: Sometimes apps or features stop working correctly. Updates fix these issues and make your phone run more smoothly.
4. **Performance Improvements**: Updates help the phone run faster and more efficiently. They can help reduce lag or fix issues with battery life.

When you keep your phone updated, you make sure that it has the latest software, which helps it perform better and stay secure.

Why Are System Updates Important?

1. **Security**: The most important reason to update your phone is security. Cybercriminals often find new ways to break into phones. By installing **security patches**, you make sure that your **Google Pixel 9 Pro** is protected against the latest threats. Without these updates, your phone might be vulnerable to malware, viruses,

or hackers.

2. **New Features**: Updates can add fun and useful new features to your phone. For example, **Android updates** often come with new ways to interact with your phone, new design options, and enhancements to your favorite apps.

3. **Bug Fixes**: No phone is perfect, and sometimes things go wrong. Maybe your phone freezes, an app crashes, or a feature stops working. A **system update** can fix bugs and improve the overall experience, ensuring that everything runs smoothly.

4. **Better Performance**: Updates can make your **Pixel 9 Pro** run faster and more efficiently. Sometimes, updates are specifically designed to improve battery life, reduce lag, or fix slowdowns that might occur over time.

5. **Compatibility**: As apps and services evolve, they often require the latest software to work correctly. If you don't update your phone, you might find that some apps stop working properly.

How to Check for System Updates on Your Google Pixel 9 Pro

Now that we understand the importance of **system updates**, let's walk through the simple steps to check for updates and install them on your **Pixel 9 Pro**.

Step 1: Open the Settings App

To start, you need to access the **Settings** menu of your phone. The **Settings** app controls all the features of your phone, and it's where you can check for system updates.

1. **Locate the Settings App**:
   ○ The **Settings** app is usually located on the **Home Screen** or in the **App Drawer**. It looks like a small gear icon. Tap it to open the **Settings** menu.

Step 2: Go to System Settings

Once you're in the **Settings** app, you need to find the part where system updates are located. This is under the **System** section.

1. **Scroll Down**:

   ○ Scroll down the **Settings** menu until you see the option labeled **System**. Tap on it to open the system-related settings.
2. **Select Software Update**:

- In the **System** section, you'll see an option called **Software Update**. Tap on it to check if a new update is available.

Step 3: Check for Updates

Once you're in the **Software Update** section, you can easily check if there's a new update available for your **Google Pixel 9 Pro**.

1. **Tap on Check for Update**:

   - You will see a button labeled **Check for Update**. Tap on it, and your phone will search for any available updates.
2. **Wait for the Check to Complete**:

   - Your phone will now connect to Google's servers to see if there are any updates. This might take a few seconds.
3. **Update Available**:

   - If an update is available, you'll see a message telling you what the update includes (e.g., new features, security fixes). Tap **Download and Install** to begin the process.
4. **No Updates**:

   - If your phone is up-to-date, you'll see a message saying that your **Pixel 9 Pro** is

already on the latest version. You can tap
Done to exit the screen.

Installing a System Update

If an update is available, the next step is to install it.
Installing updates is easy, but it's important to know a
few things before you start.

Step 1: Prepare for the Update

1. **Ensure Battery Life**:

   ○ Before starting the installation, make sure
     your **Pixel 9 Pro** has enough battery life.
     It's a good idea to have at least **50%**
     battery or connect your phone to the
     charger to prevent it from running out of
     power during the update.
2. **Connect to Wi-Fi**:

   ○ **System updates** usually require a **Wi-Fi
     connection** to download, so make sure
     your phone is connected to Wi-Fi. This is
     especially important if the update is large
     and might use a lot of data.

Step 2: Download and Install the Update

1. **Tap Download and Install**:

   - Once the update is found, tap on **Download and Install**. Your phone will start downloading the update. The speed of the download depends on your Wi-Fi connection and the size of the update.

2. **Wait for the Download**:

   - While the update is downloading, you'll see a progress bar that shows how much time is left. This may take several minutes, depending on the size of the update.

Step 3: Restart Your Phone to Install the Update

Once the update is downloaded, your phone will prompt you to restart it and install the update.

1. **Tap Restart Now**:

   - After the download is complete, you will see an option to **Restart Now** or **Install Now**. Tap this option to restart your phone and begin installing the update.

2. **Phone Will Restart**:

   - The phone will shut down and restart automatically. During this process, you will see a screen that shows the **update**

progress. It may take a few minutes to install, and the phone will restart multiple times.

3. **Phone Will Boot Up with the Latest Update**:

    o   Once the update is fully installed, your phone will boot up with the latest version of the operating system. You may see a welcome screen or a message telling you that the update was successful.

How Long Does a System Update Take?

The time it takes for a system update to download and install can vary based on a few factors:

1. **Size of the Update**:

    o   Larger updates (such as new **Android** versions) may take longer to download and install. Smaller security patches usually take less time.

2. **Internet Speed**:

    o   If you're using a fast Wi-Fi connection, the download will be quicker. If your connection is slow, it might take more time to download the update.

3. **Phone's Battery**:

   - If your battery is low, the update may take longer or even stop entirely until you connect the phone to a charger.

Typically, an update can take anywhere from **15 minutes to 1 hour** to complete, depending on the factors mentioned above.

What Happens After the Update?

Once the update is installed, your **Google Pixel 9 Pro** will restart and begin running the new software. Here are a few things you may notice after a system update:

1. **New Features**:

   - You may see new features or changes to existing ones. For example, there might be new ways to interact with apps, new settings, or improved tools for photography or security.
2. **Improved Performance**:

   - The phone might feel faster and more responsive after the update. System updates often come with performance improvements and bug fixes.

3. **New Security Patches**:

   - ○ If the update included security patches, your phone will be more secure from potential threats.
4. **App Compatibility**:

   - ○ Some apps might need to update to work with the new software. After a system update, check the **Google Play Store** for any app updates.

How to Turn On Automatic Updates

To ensure that you never miss an important system update, you can enable **automatic updates** on your **Google Pixel 9 Pro**. This way, your phone will automatically download and install updates when they become available, so you don't have to manually check for them.

Here's how to enable **automatic updates**:

1. **Go to Settings**:

   - ○ Open the **Settings** app.
2. **Tap on System**:

   - ○ Scroll down and tap on **System**.

3. **Select Software Update**:

   ○ Tap on **Software Update**.

4. **Enable Automatic Updates**:

   ○ Tap on **Automatic Updates** and toggle it
   to **On**. This will ensure that your phone
   automatically downloads and installs
   updates whenever they are available,
   without you needing to do anything.

Common Issues After Updating

While updates are generally helpful, sometimes issues
can arise after an update. Here are a few common
problems and how to fix them:

1. **Battery Draining Faster**:

   ○ After an update, you might notice that
   your battery drains faster. This could be
   because the phone is indexing or
   updating apps in the background. If this
   continues, try restarting the phone or
   adjusting **Battery Saver** settings.

2. **Slow Performance**:

   ○ Sometimes, an update can cause the
   phone to feel slower. This might happen if

the phone is downloading additional updates or apps. Give it a day or two, and if the phone is still slow, try restarting it or clearing the cache.

3. **Apps Not Working**:

   ○ After an update, some apps may not work correctly. Make sure all your apps are up-to-date by going to the **Google Play Store** and checking for updates.

4. **Update Not Installing**:

   ○ If the update fails to install, try restarting your phone and then checking for the update again. If the problem continues, you may need to troubleshoot by resetting your network settings or performing a **factory reset** (after backing up your data).

Conclusion

System updates are a vital part of keeping your **Google Pixel 9 Pro** running smoothly and securely. By regularly checking for updates, you ensure that your phone stays up to date with the latest features, security patches, and performance improvements.

In this chapter, we showed you how to check for, download, and install **system updates**. We also covered how to enable automatic updates, ensuring that your phone always has the latest software. If you run into any problems after an update, we provided tips on how to resolve them.

Now that you understand the importance of **system updates** and how to install them, your **Google Pixel 9 Pro** will continue to perform well and stay secure for years to come.

In the next chapters, we will explore more advanced settings and features to help you get the most out of your phone.

Chapter Five

Customizing Your Pixel 9 Pro

One of the great things about the **Google Pixel 9 Pro** is that you can **personalize** it to fit your unique style. From changing the **theme** to adjusting the **sound settings**, there are many ways you can make the phone truly yours. In this chapter, we will walk you through the steps to customize your **Pixel 9 Pro**'s display, sounds, and overall feel. This will help you create an experience that suits you and makes your phone easier and more enjoyable to use.

Let's dive into the steps for customizing the **Pixel 9 Pro**.

Change Themes and Wallpapers

The **theme** and **wallpaper** of your phone are two of the most obvious ways to make it feel like your own. The **theme** affects the overall color scheme of your phone, and the **wallpaper** is the image or design that appears on your **Home Screen** and **Lock Screen**.

Changing the Theme

Your **Pixel 9 Pro** allows you to change the **theme**, which adjusts the colors used in the phone's interface. This includes the background colors, button colors, and how text appears on your phone.

To change the **theme**, follow these steps:

1. **Open the Settings App**:

   ○ Tap the **Settings icon** (which looks like a small gear) on your **Home Screen** or **App Drawer** to open the **Settings** menu.

2. **Go to Display Settings**:

   ○ In the **Settings** menu, scroll down and tap on **Display**. This will open the display settings where you can adjust the brightness, screen resolution, and other visual settings.

3. **Tap on Theme**:

   ○ In the **Display** menu, look for an option called **Theme**. Tap on it to see the different theme options available.

4. **Choose a Theme**:

   ○ You will have different **theme** choices, such as **Light** and **Dark** themes. Choose the one that best fits your preferences.
      - **Light Theme**: This is the default theme, with white backgrounds and dark text. It is best for bright environments.

- **Dark Theme**: This theme changes the background to a dark color, usually black or dark gray, with light-colored text. It's easier on your eyes in low-light environments and can save battery life on **OLED displays** like the one on your **Pixel 9 Pro**.

5. **Confirm Your Selection**:

   - After selecting the theme you prefer, tap **OK** or **Apply** to confirm. The phone will immediately change to the selected theme.

Setting Your Wallpaper

Changing the **wallpaper** is another fun and easy way to personalize your **Google Pixel 9 Pro**. The **wallpaper** is the background image that appears on your **Home Screen** and **Lock Screen**. You can choose from pre-installed wallpapers, photos from your own gallery, or even download new wallpapers from the internet.

To set your **wallpaper**, follow these steps:

1. **Tap and Hold on the Home Screen**:

   - On your **Home Screen**, tap and hold on an empty space (where there are no app icons or widgets). After holding it for a moment, the **Home Screen options** will appear.

2. **Select Wallpapers**:

   ○ In the **Home Screen options**, tap on **Wallpapers**. This will take you to the wallpaper settings, where you can choose your preferred background image.

3. **Choose a Wallpaper**:

   ○ You will see several options for wallpapers:
      ■ **Live Wallpapers**: These are moving or interactive wallpapers. Tap on a live wallpaper if you want a dynamic background.
      ■ **Pre-installed Wallpapers**: Your phone comes with a variety of default wallpapers, including nature images, abstract designs, and more.
      ■ **Photos**: If you have pictures on your phone, you can choose one as your wallpaper. Tap on **My Photos** to select an image from your gallery.
      ■ **Online Wallpapers**: If you want something unique, you can search for new wallpapers online. There

are many websites and apps that
offer free wallpapers.

4. **Set the Wallpaper**:

    ○   After you choose your wallpaper, tap **Set
        Wallpaper**. You'll be asked whether you
        want to set it for your **Home Screen**,
        Lock Screen, or both. Select the option
        you prefer, then tap **Set**.

5. **Preview Your Wallpaper**:

    ○   You'll be able to preview how the
        wallpaper looks on your **Home Screen**
        and **Lock Screen**. If you're happy with
        your choice, tap **Done** to save it.

Adjust Notifications and Sounds

Now that you've customized the **theme** and **wallpaper**,
let's move on to adjusting the **sound** settings. The **Pixel
9 Pro** allows you to control the sounds for things like
ringtones, **notifications**, and **vibration**. You can make
sure your phone sounds just the way you want it.

Adjusting Ringtone Volume

To adjust the **ringtone volume**, which controls how loud
your phone rings when you receive a call, follow these
steps:

1. **Open the Settings App**:

   ○ Open the **Settings** app from your **Home Screen** or **App Drawer**.

2. **Go to Sound Settings**:

   ○ Scroll down and tap on **Sound**. This section contains all the sound-related settings for your phone.

3. **Adjust the Ringtone Volume**:

   ○ Under the **Sound** settings, you'll see a slider for **Ringtone**. Move the slider left or right to adjust the volume of your phone's ringtone. You can test it by tapping on **Play** to hear how the ringtone sounds at the current volume.

4. **Set Ringtone**:

   ○ Below the **Ringtone volume** slider, you'll see the option to **Select ringtone**. Tap on it to choose a different ringtone for incoming calls. You can choose from the pre-installed ringtones or any music file you have on your phone.

Adjusting Vibration

The **vibration** settings control how your phone vibrates for notifications, calls, or when you touch the screen.

1. **Go to Vibration Settings**:

   o   In the **Sound** menu, scroll down to find **Vibration**. Tap on it to adjust how the phone vibrates when you receive a notification or call.

2. **Turn Vibration On or Off**:

   o   You can choose to turn the vibration on or off for different actions, like incoming calls, notifications, or alarms. Simply toggle the switches for each option based on your preference.

Set Do Not Disturb

The **Do Not Disturb** feature is useful when you need some quiet time. It silences notifications, calls, and alerts. You can customize it to allow only certain people or apps to interrupt you.

1. **Go to Do Not Disturb Settings**:

   o   Open the **Settings** app and tap on **Sound**. Then, select **Do Not Disturb**.

2. **Activate Do Not Disturb**:

- Tap on the toggle to turn **Do Not Disturb** on. Once activated, your phone will silence calls, messages, and notifications. You can also schedule it to turn on automatically at certain times.

3. **Customize Exceptions**:

- Tap on **Allow Exceptions** to choose who or what can break through **Do Not Disturb**. For example, you can allow calls from certain contacts or let alarm sounds pass through even when **Do Not Disturb** is on.

4. **Set a Schedule**:

- You can also set a schedule for **Do Not Disturb**. For example, you can make it turn on automatically every night at a certain time and turn off in the morning. Tap on **Turn On Automatically** and set your preferred schedule.

Advanced Sound Settings

There are additional sound settings you can customize to make your phone's audio experience perfect.

Sound for Notifications

1. **Change Notification Sounds**:

    - Go to **Settings > Sound** and scroll down to **Advanced**. Here, you can select different sounds for your **notifications** and **messages**.
    - Tap on **Default Notification Sound** to choose a new sound. You can pick from pre-installed sounds or choose a custom sound from your files.

2. **Set Ringtone for Specific Contacts**:

    - You can assign different ringtones to specific contacts. Go to **Contacts**, select the contact you want, tap on **Edit**, and choose a ringtone just for that contact.

Additional Customization Options

There are several more ways you can customize the **Pixel 9 Pro** to make it fit your preferences. Here are some other options to consider:

1. **Change Icon Shape**:

    - Go to **Settings > Display > Icon Shape** and choose a shape that suits you, like round, squircle, or squared icons.

2. **Night Light**:

   - You can reduce blue light exposure by enabling **Night Light**. Go to **Settings > Display > Night Light** to enable it. This makes the screen warmer, which can be easier on your eyes, especially at night.

3. **Display Size**:

   - To make text and icons larger or smaller, go to **Settings > Display > Display Size**. Adjust the slider to make everything easier to see.

4. **Font Size**:

   - If you find text hard to read, you can change the font size by going to **Settings > Display > Font Size**. Use the slider to make the text bigger or smaller.

Conclusion

Personalizing your **Google Pixel 9 Pro** is simple and fun. Whether you're changing the **theme**, adjusting the **sounds**, or customizing the **wallpaper**, these settings allow you to create an experience that fits your style. From fine-tuning notification sounds to setting up **Do Not Disturb**, your **Pixel 9 Pro** can be perfectly tuned to meet your needs.

By following the steps in this chapter, you now know how to make your phone look and sound exactly the way you want. Don't forget to explore additional customization options in **Settings** to make the phone even more tailored to you.

In the next chapters, we'll continue exploring more advanced features of your **Google Pixel 9 Pro**, such as security settings and system performance. Let's keep customizing and optimizing your phone for the best experience!

Organizing the Home Screen and Using Gesture Controls

Your **Google Pixel 9 Pro** is not only a powerful phone but also one that allows you to personalize how it looks and how you interact with it. Organizing your **Home Screen** and setting up **gesture controls** are two key steps to making your phone even easier and more enjoyable to use. In this chapter, we will walk you through the steps of organizing your **Home Screen**, creating **app folders**, adding **widgets**, and setting up useful **gesture controls** like **Quick Tap** and **Flip to Shhh**.

Let's start by customizing your **Home Screen** and then dive into the powerful **gesture controls** that your **Google Pixel 9 Pro** offers.

Organizing the Home Screen

The **Home Screen** is the place where you spend most of your time with your phone. Organizing it efficiently can make it much easier to access your apps and find everything you need quickly. Let's explore how you can create **app folders**, use **widgets**, and customize your **Home Screen**.

Creating App Folders

Over time, you may install many apps on your phone. While this is great, it can also make your **Home Screen** look cluttered and hard to navigate. Fortunately, you can organize your apps into **folders** to keep things neat and tidy.

App folders group related apps together, making it easier to find them when you need them. For example, you can create a folder for **social media apps** like **Facebook**, **Instagram**, and **Twitter** or group all your **shopping apps** together.

To create an **app folder**, follow these simple steps:

1. **Tap and Hold an App Icon:**

   ○ Go to your **Home Screen** and find the app you want to move into a folder.
   ○ Tap and hold on the app icon for a moment. After a second, the app icon will

begin to wiggle or give you the option to move it.

2. **Drag the App Over Another App**:

   - While still holding the app icon, drag it over another app that you want to group it with. When you release the app, you will see that the two apps have automatically been grouped into a folder.
   - The **folder** will appear on your **Home Screen**, and it will display both apps inside.

3. **Name the Folder**:

   - Once the folder is created, it will have a default name, like **"Social"** or **"Games"**. To rename the folder, tap on the folder, and you will see the current name at the top.
   - Tap on the name to change it to something more specific. For example, you could name the folder **"Social Media"** or **"Shopping"**.

4. **Add More Apps to the Folder**:

   - To add more apps to the folder, tap and hold the app you want to add. Then, drag it into the folder. Release it inside, and it will now be part of the folder.

5. **Remove Apps from the Folder**:

- If you want to remove an app from the folder, open the folder and tap and hold the app you want to remove.
- Drag it out of the folder and drop it onto the **Home Screen**. The folder will remain, but the app will now be outside the folder.

6. **Delete a Folder**:

- If you want to delete a folder, you first need to remove all the apps from it. Once the folder is empty, it will disappear automatically.

By using **app folders**, you can organize your **Home Screen** into clear categories, making it easier to find apps and keep your phone tidy.

Using Widgets

Widgets are small, interactive apps that display useful information directly on your **Home Screen**. They are a great way to make your phone more functional, as they allow you to access important data quickly without opening an app. For example, you can add a **weather widget**, a **calendar widget**, or a **news widget** to your **Home Screen**.

Here's how to add and use **widgets** on your **Google Pixel 9 Pro**:

1. **Tap and Hold on the Home Screen**:

   - On your **Home Screen**, tap and hold an empty space (where there are no app icons or widgets). This will bring up the **Home Screen options**.

2. **Select Widgets**:

   - From the options that appear, tap on **Widgets**. This will open a list of all available widgets that you can add to your **Home Screen**.

3. **Browse and Choose a Widget**:

   - You will see a variety of widgets for different apps. For example, you can add a **weather widget** to see the current temperature or a **calendar widget** to see your upcoming events. Scroll through the list and choose the widget you want to add.

4. **Tap and Hold the Widget**:

   - Once you find a widget you like, tap and hold on it. Then, drag it to an empty space on your **Home Screen**.

5. **Resize the Widget**:

   - Some widgets can be resized to take up more or less space on your **Home Screen**. After adding the widget, tap and hold it, then drag the corners to make it bigger or smaller.

6. **Remove a Widget**:

   ○ If you want to remove a widget, tap and hold it on the **Home Screen**, and then drag it to the **Remove** icon at the top of the screen (it looks like a trash can). Release it to delete the widget.

Some popular widgets to consider adding to your **Pixel 9 Pro** include:

- **Weather Widget**: Shows the current weather conditions.
- **Google Calendar Widget**: Displays your upcoming events.
- **News Widget**: Shows the latest headlines and news articles.
- **Clock Widget**: Displays the time or includes a world clock.

Gesture Controls

The **Google Pixel 9 Pro** is designed to be fast and easy to use, and **gesture controls** play a big part in that. Instead of using physical buttons, you can perform various actions on your phone using simple gestures. For example, you can **Quick Tap** to launch an app or feature, or **Flip to Shhh** to silence the phone when you flip it over. These gestures help you interact with your phone faster and more efficiently.

Let's explore how to enable and configure some of the key **gesture controls** on your **Google Pixel 9 Pro**.

Quick Tap Gesture

The **Quick Tap** gesture lets you quickly perform an action by double-tapping the back of your phone. You can use **Quick Tap** to launch an app, take a screenshot, or start a Google Assistant command. It's a convenient gesture that saves you time when you need to access something quickly.

Here's how to enable and configure the **Quick Tap** gesture:

1. **Open the Settings App**:

    ○ Tap the **Settings icon** to open the **Settings** menu.
2. **Go to System**:

    ○ Scroll down and tap on **System**.
3. **Select Gestures**:

    ○ In the **System** section, tap on **Gestures** to open the gesture settings.

4. **Enable Quick Tap**:

   ○ Look for the **Quick Tap** option. Toggle the switch to turn it on.

5. **Configure Quick Tap Action**:

   ○ Once enabled, tap on **Quick Tap** to choose what action you want to assign to the gesture. You can choose from several options, such as:
     - **Take Screenshot**: Double-tap the back of the phone to take a screenshot.
     - **Launch Google Assistant**: Double-tap to activate **Google Assistant** and ask questions or issue commands.
     - **Open an App**: You can assign a specific app to open when you perform the **Quick Tap** gesture.

6. **Test Quick Tap**:

   ○ Once you've set up your **Quick Tap** gesture, test it by double-tapping the back of your phone. It should perform the action you selected.

Flip to Shhh Gesture

The **Flip to Shhh** gesture allows you to quickly silence your phone by simply flipping it over. This is a handy feature when you're in a meeting, in class, or just need some quiet time. When you flip your phone over, it automatically activates **Do Not Disturb** mode, preventing notifications, calls, and alerts from disturbing you.

Here's how to enable and configure the **Flip to Shhh** gesture:

1. **Open the Settings App**:

   ○ Tap the **Settings icon** on your **Home Screen** or **App Drawer**.
2. **Go to System**:

   ○ Scroll down and tap on **System**.
3. **Select Gestures**:

   ○ Tap on **Gestures** in the **System** section.
4. **Enable Flip to Shhh**:

   ○ Find and toggle the **Flip to Shhh** option to enable it.
5. **Test Flip to Shhh**:

   ○ Once activated, try flipping your **Pixel 9 Pro** over onto its back. You should feel the phone vibrate briefly, indicating that

Do Not Disturb mode has been activated.

6. **Configure Do Not Disturb**:

    ○   If you want to customize what happens when **Do Not Disturb** is turned on, go to **Settings > Sound > Do Not Disturb**. Here, you can choose which notifications are silenced and who can still contact you while in **Do Not Disturb** mode.

Other Useful Gestures

In addition to **Quick Tap** and **Flip to Shhh**, your **Pixel 9 Pro** includes other helpful gestures that can make it easier to navigate your phone.

1. **Lift to Check Phone**:

    ○   When you lift your phone, the screen will automatically light up, so you can quickly check notifications or unlock the phone with your face or fingerprint.
    ○   To enable this, go to **Settings > Display > Lift to Check Phone** and toggle it on.

2. **Swipe for Notifications**:

    ○   To access your notifications, swipe down from the top of the screen. This will bring down the notification shade, allowing you to view and interact with notifications, adjust settings, and more.

3. **Swipe for Quick Settings**:

   ○ Swipe down from the top of the screen to access **Quick Settings**, where you can toggle things like **Wi-Fi**, **Bluetooth**, and **Do Not Disturb**.

Conclusion

In this chapter, we've covered how to organize your **Home Screen** by creating **app folders**, adding **widgets**, and customizing the overall layout of your phone. We also explored how to enable and configure **gesture controls** like **Quick Tap** and **Flip to Shhh**, which make using your **Google Pixel 9 Pro** faster and more efficient.

By following these simple steps, you can personalize your phone to work the way you want, with everything easily accessible and tailored to your needs.

In the next chapters, we will explore more advanced features and settings of your **Pixel 9 Pro**, so stay tuned for even more ways to optimize your phone and make the most out of its features.

Chapter Six

Navigating Android 14 Features on Your Google Pixel 9 Pro

In this chapter, we will guide you through the new features of **Android 14** on your **Google Pixel 9 Pro**. Android 14 brings several improvements and tools designed to help you get the most out of your phone. Whether you want to manage your screen time, ensure your privacy, or personalize **Google Assistant**, this chapter will show you how to make the most of these features to enhance your experience.

Let's dive into the **Digital Wellbeing**, **Privacy Settings**, and **Google Assistant** features in **Android 14**.

Set Up Digital Wellbeing

With **Digital Wellbeing**, Android helps you find a balance between technology and life. This feature is designed to help you manage screen time, limit distractions, and make sure that technology doesn't interfere with your personal time. You can use **Digital Wellbeing** to monitor how much time you spend on apps, set **screen time limits**, and even take breaks with features like **Focus Mode**.

Let's explore how to set up and use **Digital Wellbeing**.

Step 1: Access Digital Wellbeing Settings

1. **Open the Settings App**:

   ○ From your **Home Screen** or **App Drawer**, tap on the **Settings** app.

2. **Go to Digital Wellbeing & Parental Controls**:

   ○ In the **Settings** menu, scroll down and find **Digital Wellbeing & Parental Controls**. Tap on it to open the **Digital Wellbeing** settings.

Step 2: Set Screen Time Limits

One of the key features of **Digital Wellbeing** is the ability to set **screen time limits** for specific apps. This helps you monitor and reduce your screen time to make sure you're not spending too much time on apps, especially those that might be distracting.

1. **Tap on Dashboard**:

   ○ Under **Digital Wellbeing & Parental Controls**, tap on **Dashboard**. This will show a list of all the apps you use, along with the time spent on each one.

2. **Set Time Limits**:

- For any app you want to limit, tap on the **hourglass icon** next to the app. A slider will appear, allowing you to set a **screen time limit** for that app. You can set a limit for up to **24 hours**.

3. **Tap Done**:

- After you set the time limit, tap **Done**. The app will now notify you when you've reached the screen time limit, helping you manage how much time you spend on it.

Step 3: Focus Mode

Focus Mode is a tool that allows you to silence distracting apps so that you can focus on what really matters. This feature is great for when you need to stay focused at work, study, or during personal time.

1. **Go to Focus Mode**:

- In the **Digital Wellbeing & Parental Controls** menu, tap on **Focus Mode**.

2. **Select Apps to Silence**:

- You'll see a list of apps that you can silence. Tap on the apps you want to limit (such as social media or games) and select **Turn On** to start **Focus Mode**.

3. **Set a Time for Focus Mode**:

- You can set **Focus Mode** to last for a specific period, or you can turn it on for the entire day. When you turn on **Focus Mode**, the selected apps will be silenced, and you won't receive notifications from them.

4. **Exit Focus Mode**:

- When you're done, you can exit **Focus Mode** by going back to the **Focus Mode** settings and selecting **Turn Off**. Your apps will now start sending notifications again.

Privacy Settings

Your **privacy** is important, and **Android 14** has added several ways to control what apps can access on your phone. You can manage app permissions, enable **Location History**, and control **Activity Controls** to ensure that your data is only shared when you want it to be.

Let's go through how to manage your **privacy settings**.

Step 1: Manage App Permissions

Apps need permission to access certain features on your phone, such as your **camera**, **microphone**,

location, and **storage**. Android 14 lets you control what permissions each app can use, giving you full control over your data.

1. **Open the Settings App**:

   ○ Start by opening the **Settings** app on your **Pixel 9 Pro**.

2. **Go to Privacy**:

   ○ Scroll down and tap on **Privacy** in the **Settings** menu.

3. **Select Permission Manager**:

   ○ In the **Privacy** section, tap on **Permission Manager**. This will show a list of all the different types of data, like **Location**, **Camera**, **Microphone**, and **Storage**.

4. **Choose a Permission Type**:

   ○ For example, if you want to control which apps have access to your **location**, tap on **Location**. You will see all the apps that have requested access to your location.

5. **Adjust Permissions**:

   ○ Tap on any app in the list to adjust its permission. You can choose from:

- **Allow**: The app can access that data (e.g., location, camera).
- **Deny**: The app cannot access that data.
- **Ask Every Time**: The app will ask for permission each time it needs access to that data.

6. **Repeat for Other Permissions**:

   ○ You can repeat these steps for other permissions like **Camera**, **Microphone**, and **Storage**. This gives you full control over what data apps can access on your phone.

Step 2: Enable Location History

If you want a more personalized experience, you can enable **Location History** to track your visits to places and help improve services like **Google Maps** and **Google Assistant**.

1. **Open the Settings App**:

   ○ Go to **Settings** on your phone.

2. **Tap on Google**:

   ○ Scroll down and tap on **Google** to open **Google Settings**.

3. **Go to Location**:

- In **Google Settings**, tap on **Location** to adjust location-related features.
4. **Enable Location History**:

- In the **Location** section, you will see **Location History**. Toggle it to **On** if it's not already enabled. This allows Google to track your location history and provide more personalized suggestions.
5. **Manage Location History**:

- You can view your **Location History** at any time by going to **Google Maps**. If you ever want to delete your location history, you can do so by visiting the **Location History** settings.

Step 3: Enable Activity Controls

Activity Controls allow you to control what kind of data Google can use to personalize your experience. This includes things like **web and app activity**, **device information**, and **voice and audio recordings**.

1. **Open the Settings App**:

- Open **Settings** from the **Home Screen**.
2. **Tap on Google**:

- Scroll down and tap on **Google** in the **Settings** menu.

3. **Go to Activity Controls**:

   - In **Google Settings**, tap on **Activity Controls**.

4. **Manage Activity Data**:

   - Here, you can choose what types of activity you want Google to store, such as:
     - **Web & App Activity**: Data from your web searches and activities in apps.
     - **Location History**: Data about the places you've visited.
     - **YouTube History**: The videos you've watched on **YouTube**.

5. **Turn Off Activity Data**:

   - You can choose to turn off **Activity Controls** for any of the data types listed above. This will prevent Google from saving that activity to personalize your experience.

Google Assistant: Set Up and Personalize

Google Assistant is one of the most powerful tools on your **Pixel 9 Pro**. It allows you to use voice commands to do things like check the weather, send texts, set reminders, and control your smart devices. You can also personalize **Google Assistant** to make it work better for you.

Let's look at how to set up and personalize **Google Assistant** on your phone.

Step 1: Access Google Assistant Settings

1. **Open the Settings App:**

   ○ Tap the **Settings** icon on your **Home Screen** or **App Drawer**.
2. **Go to Google Settings:**

   ○ Scroll down and tap on **Google** to open **Google Settings**.
3. **Tap on Search, Assistant & Voice:**

   ○ In **Google Settings**, tap on **Search, Assistant & Voice** to find the settings for **Google Assistant**.
4. **Tap on Google Assistant:**

   ○ Tap on **Google Assistant** to access the **Assistant** settings.

Step 2: Set Up Google Assistant

1. **Enable Google Assistant:**

- If **Google Assistant** is not enabled, toggle the switch to turn it on. You will be guided through a quick setup process to activate the assistant.
2. **Personalize Google Assistant**:

- After activating **Google Assistant**, you can personalize it by adjusting settings such as:
  - **Voice Match**: Train Google Assistant to recognize your voice so it can respond when you say "Hey Google."
  - **Assistant Voice**: Choose the voice of your **Google Assistant**. You can select from different accents and genders.
  - **Personal Results**: Allow **Google Assistant** to give personalized results based on your calendar, contacts, and other data.

Step 3: Use Google Assistant

1. **Activate Google Assistant**:

- You can activate **Google Assistant** in several ways:
  - **Say "Hey Google"**: This will activate the assistant without needing to press anything.

- **Press and hold the Home button**: This is another way to bring up the assistant if you prefer using the button.
- **Use the Google Assistant icon**: If you have a **Google Assistant** icon on your **Home Screen**, simply tap it to start interacting with the assistant.

2. **Ask Questions or Give Commands**:

   - You can ask **Google Assistant** questions or give it commands like:
     - "What's the weather today?"
     - "Set a reminder for my meeting at 3 PM."
     - "Send a text to Mom saying I'll be home in 10 minutes."

Conclusion

In this chapter, we explored the new features of **Android 14** on your **Google Pixel 9 Pro**, including **Digital Wellbeing**, **Privacy Settings**, and **Google Assistant**. We showed you how to set up **screen time limits**, enable **Focus Mode**, manage app permissions, and personalize **Google Assistant** to work better for you.

By following these steps, you can make sure your **Google Pixel 9 Pro** is not only optimized for your needs but also secure and personalized to your liking.

In the next chapters, we will explore more features and settings to help you get the most out of your phone.

Chapter Seven

AI Features and Integration on Your Google Pixel 9 Pro

The **Google Pixel 9 Pro** is a phone packed with advanced **AI features** that can make your life easier and more efficient. These features are designed to handle everyday tasks with ease, helping you get things done faster and more accurately. From voice commands with **Google Assistant** to smart **camera tools** that enhance your photos, the **Pixel 9 Pro** offers powerful tools powered by artificial intelligence. In this chapter, we will explore how you can use these **AI features** to improve your experience with the phone.

Use Google Assistant

One of the most prominent **AI features** on your **Google Pixel 9 Pro** is **Google Assistant**. This voice-activated assistant allows you to interact with your phone using only your voice. Whether you want to ask questions, set reminders, control your smart devices, or get information, **Google Assistant** is here to help.

Let's break down how to activate and use **Google Assistant** effectively.

Activating Google Assistant

You can activate **Google Assistant** in two easy ways:

1. **Say "Hey Google"**:

   - This is the most common way to activate **Google Assistant**. Simply say the phrase, **"Hey Google,"** followed by your question or command. For example:
     - "Hey Google, what's the weather today?"
     - "Hey Google, set a reminder for 3 PM."
2. Once you say **"Hey Google,"** the assistant will activate, and you can ask it anything you want.

3. **Hold the Home Button**:

   - If you prefer using the **Home button**, simply **press and hold the Home button** for a few seconds. The **Google Assistant** interface will pop up, allowing you to ask questions or give commands.

Using Google Assistant

Once **Google Assistant** is activated, you can use it for a variety of tasks. Here are some examples of what you can do with **Google Assistant**:

1. **Ask Questions**:

    o   You can ask **Google Assistant** almost anything. Whether it's about the weather, news, or general information, **Google Assistant** can provide you with answers in seconds.
        ▪   Example: "Hey Google, what's the capital of France?"
2. **Set Reminders**:

    o   You can use **Google Assistant** to set reminders so that you never forget important tasks.
        ▪   Example: "Hey Google, remind me to call Mom at 4 PM."
3. **Send Messages or Make Calls**:

    o   You can dictate text messages or make calls hands-free.
        ▪   Example: "Hey Google, send a message to John saying I'll be late."
4. **Control Smart Devices**:

    o   If you have smart devices at home, you can control them using **Google Assistant**. You can adjust your thermostat, turn on lights, or even play music, all with just your voice.

- Example: "Hey Google, turn off the lights."
- Example: "Hey Google, play some music."

5. **Set Alarms and Timers**:

   - You can set alarms or timers for cooking, exercise, or reminders.
     - Example: "Hey Google, set a timer for 20 minutes."

6. **Get Directions**:

   - **Google Assistant** can also help you with navigation, providing turn-by-turn directions, traffic updates, and more.
     - Example: "Hey Google, get directions to the nearest coffee shop."

Personalizing Google Assistant

You can personalize **Google Assistant** to suit your preferences and make it more effective. Here's how to customize it:

1. **Change Assistant Voice**:

- **Google Assistant** offers different voices that you can select from. To change the voice, follow these steps:
  - Open the **Settings** app.
  - Tap on **Google**.
  - Select **Search, Assistant & Voice**.
  - Tap on **Google Assistant**.
  - Select **Assistant Voice** and choose your preferred voice.

2. **Voice Match**:

  - **Voice Match** allows **Google Assistant** to recognize your voice. This means that only you can access your personal information through voice commands.
    - To enable **Voice Match**, go to **Settings > Google > Search, Assistant & Voice > Google Assistant** and turn on **Voice Match**. Follow the instructions to teach the assistant to recognize your voice.

3. **Personal Results**:

  - If you want **Google Assistant** to give personalized results (like showing your calendar events or personal reminders), you can enable **Personal Results**. To do this, go to **Settings > Google > Search,**

Assistant & Voice > Google Assistant,
then toggle on **Personal Results**.

Enhance Photos with AI

The **Google Pixel 9 Pro** comes with AI-powered tools in its **camera** that can automatically enhance your photos. These tools help improve the quality of your images by fixing lighting, focusing on the right areas, and even suggesting edits.

Let's look at how the AI camera tools work and how you can use them to enhance your photos.

AI-Powered Camera Features

The **Pixel 9 Pro** camera has several AI tools built-in to make your photos look better automatically. These tools include features like **Auto-Enhance**, **Night Sight**, and **Portrait Mode**, which are designed to improve the quality of your pictures.

1. **Auto-Enhance**:

   ○ **Auto-Enhance** is an AI feature that automatically analyzes your photos and adjusts the lighting, contrast, and colors to make them look better. This feature is enabled by default, so when you take a photo, the AI automatically enhances it without you having to do anything.

2. **Night Sight**:

   ○ **Night Sight** is a powerful tool for taking clear photos in low-light conditions. It uses AI to increase the brightness and sharpness of your pictures, even in the dark. To use **Night Sight**, simply open the camera app, tap on **Night Sight**, and snap a photo in a low-light environment. The AI will do the rest.

3. **Portrait Mode**:

   ○ **Portrait Mode** uses AI to blur the background and keep your subject sharp and in focus. This feature mimics the effect of a professional camera and makes your subject stand out. Just open the camera app, select **Portrait Mode**, and position the subject in the frame. The AI will automatically adjust the background to create the perfect bokeh effect.

4. **Lens Suggestions**:

   ○ The **Google Pixel 9 Pro** camera uses **Lens Suggestions** to recommend the best camera lens (like **wide-angle** or **telephoto**) for your shot. The AI automatically detects the scene and suggests the most appropriate lens for the best result.

5. **AI Image Enhancement**:

   ○ After taking a photo, the **Google Pixel 9 Pro** may offer suggestions for edits, such as adjusting exposure, brightness, or contrast. You can apply these changes directly from the **Google Photos** app, or let the AI make automatic improvements for you.

Editing Photos with AI

Once your photo is taken, you can enhance it further using the **Google Photos** app, which includes AI-powered editing tools. These tools are designed to help you make quick improvements to your images with just a few taps.

1. **Auto-Enhance**:

   ○ If you want to improve your photos after they are taken, open the photo in **Google Photos**, and tap **Edit**. The app will automatically suggest edits, such as adjusting the brightness, saturation, and contrast to make the photo look better.

2. **Adjust Lighting**:

    ○ **Google Photos** uses AI to analyze the lighting in your photos and make adjustments. Tap **Adjust** to manually change the **exposure, brightness,** and **shadows**.

3. **Filters**:

    ○ AI-based filters are available in **Google Photos**, giving your photos a new look. You can choose from a variety of filters that adjust the overall color tone of the photo. These filters are powered by AI, which ensures that the photo looks natural and balanced.

4. **Blur Background**:

    ○ If you want to enhance the focus of your subject, use the **Blur** feature in **Google Photos**. This tool lets you blur the background of your photo, creating a depth-of-field effect similar to **Portrait Mode**.

Pixel Screenshots

Taking screenshots on your **Google Pixel 9 Pro** is simple, but **Pixel 9 Pro** offers some extra features to make screenshots even more useful. You can take screenshots, annotate them, and even search through them later using keywords. This is powered by **AI**, which helps you manage your screenshots.

How to Take a Screenshot

Taking a screenshot is as easy as pressing a combination of buttons:

1. **Press the Power Button and Volume Down Button**:

   - To take a screenshot, press the **Power button** and **Volume Down button** at the same time for a quick moment. Your phone will capture what's on the screen and show you a preview of the screenshot.
2. **Tap on the Preview to Edit or Share**:

   - After taking the screenshot, a preview will appear at the bottom of the screen. You can tap on the preview to **edit** or **share** the screenshot.

Annotating Screenshots

You can add text, drawings, or highlights to your screenshots, making them more informative or fun.

1. **Tap on the Edit Icon**:

     ○ After taking a screenshot, tap the **Edit icon** (pencil) to start editing the screenshot.

2. **Add Text, Drawings, or Shapes**:

     ○ Use the **text tool** to add labels, or use the **drawing tool** to highlight or underline important parts of the screenshot.

3. **Save or Share**:

     ○ Once you're done editing, you can save the annotated screenshot or share it with others via **email, messaging apps**, or social media.

Search Through Screenshots

One of the powerful features of **Google Pixel 9 Pro** is the ability to search through your screenshots using **AI**. Google's **AI** can recognize text and objects in your screenshots, making it easier to find the exact image you need.

1. **Open Google Photos**:

- All of your screenshots will be saved in **Google Photos**. Open the app to see your photos, including screenshots.

2. **Use the Search Bar:**

   - At the top of **Google Photos**, there's a **search bar** where you can type keywords to find specific screenshots. Google's **AI** will recognize objects or text in the screenshots and show relevant results.

3. **Search by Keyword:**

   - For example, if you took a screenshot of a restaurant menu, you can search for keywords like "menu" or "restaurant," and **Google Photos** will show you the screenshot even if you don't remember where you saved it.

Conclusion

Your **Google Pixel 9 Pro** is full of powerful **AI features** designed to make your life easier. Whether it's **Google Assistant** helping you with voice commands, **AI-powered camera tools** enhancing your photos, or the ability to take and annotate **screenshots**, these features allow you to interact with your phone more efficiently.

By learning how to use these **AI features**, you can take full advantage of your phone's capabilities. From personalizing your assistant to editing your photos with AI, these tools make your **Pixel 9 Pro** smarter and more responsive.

In the next chapters, we will continue to explore even more advanced features, such as **security settings**, **customization options**, and tips to improve **battery life** and **performance**.

Chapter Eight

Connectivity and Communication Features on Your Google Pixel 9 Pro

Your **Google Pixel 9 Pro** is equipped with several powerful connectivity and communication features that allow you to stay connected to the world around you. Whether you need to connect to **Wi-Fi, Bluetooth devices**, or set up **Google Meet** for video calls, this chapter will guide you through all the communication and connectivity tools available on your phone. We will also explore emergency features like **Satellite SOS** for safe communication in critical situations. Let's dive in and learn how to make the most of these features.

Connect to Wi-Fi and Bluetooth

Wi-Fi and Bluetooth are two essential ways to connect to the internet and wirelessly transfer data or use devices. On your **Google Pixel 9 Pro**, connecting to Wi-Fi and Bluetooth is simple and fast. Here's how to connect to both.

Connecting to Wi-Fi

Wi-Fi allows you to access the internet without using mobile data. It is a more stable and faster connection, so it's always a good idea to connect to Wi-Fi when possible, especially at home or in public places like cafes.

To connect to a **Wi-Fi network** on your **Pixel 9 Pro**, follow these steps:

1. **Open the Settings App**:

   o Tap the **Settings** icon from your **Home Screen** or **App Drawer** to open the **Settings** menu.

2. **Go to Wi-Fi Settings**:

   o In the **Settings** menu, scroll down and tap on **Wi-Fi**. This will take you to the Wi-Fi settings where you can see all the available networks.

3. **Turn On Wi-Fi**:

   o If **Wi-Fi** is not already turned on, tap the **toggle switch** at the top to turn on Wi-Fi.

4. **Choose a Network**:

   o After enabling Wi-Fi, your phone will scan for available networks. A list of Wi-Fi networks will appear.

   o Select the Wi-Fi network you want to connect to. If it's a secured network, you will be prompted to enter the **Wi-Fi password**.

5. **Enter the Password**:

   o If required, enter the password for the selected network. Be careful to enter it correctly. Once you enter the password, tap **Connect**.

6. **Connected to Wi-Fi**:

   o After a few seconds, your **Google Pixel 9 Pro** will connect to the Wi-Fi network. You will see a Wi-Fi icon in the top-right corner of the screen, indicating that you are connected.

Troubleshooting Wi-Fi Connection

If you're having trouble connecting to a Wi-Fi network, here are some steps to troubleshoot:

1. **Make sure Wi-Fi is turned on**: Double-check that Wi-Fi is enabled in the **Settings**.
2. **Check the password**: Ensure that you entered the correct password for the network.
3. **Restart your phone**: Sometimes, simply restarting your phone can solve connection issues.
4. **Restart the router**: If other devices are also having trouble connecting to the Wi-Fi, try restarting the router.

5. **Move closer to the router**: If the signal is weak, moving closer to the Wi-Fi router may help.

Connecting to Bluetooth Devices

Bluetooth allows you to wirelessly connect to other devices, such as headphones, speakers, or even your car's infotainment system. It's an essential feature for hands-free communication, streaming music, or using wireless accessories.

Here's how to connect a Bluetooth device to your **Pixel 9 Pro**:

1. **Open the Settings App**:

   - Open the **Settings** app from the **Home Screen** or **App Drawer**.
2. **Go to Bluetooth Settings**:

   - Scroll down and tap on **Bluetooth** in the **Settings** menu.
3. **Turn On Bluetooth**:

   - If **Bluetooth** is not already enabled, tap the **toggle switch** at the top to turn it on.
4. **Scan for Devices**:

   - Your phone will automatically start scanning for available Bluetooth devices nearby. Make sure the device you want to connect to (like headphones or speakers) is in pairing mode.

5. **Select Your Device**:

   - Once your phone detects the available device, it will appear in the list of available devices. Tap on the device you want to pair with.

6. **Pair the Device**:

   - If prompted, confirm the pairing by tapping **Yes** or **Pair**. Some devices may also require a **PIN** or **passcode**. Enter the code if needed.

7. **Connected to Bluetooth**:

   - After pairing, the Bluetooth device will be connected, and you can start using it for audio, calls, or other functions.

Troubleshooting Bluetooth Connection

If you experience issues with connecting to Bluetooth, try the following steps:

1. **Ensure Bluetooth is enabled**: Make sure that Bluetooth is turned on in the **Settings**.
2. **Check that the Bluetooth device is in pairing mode**: Ensure the device you are connecting to is ready to pair.

3. **Restart Bluetooth**: Try turning Bluetooth off and on again, then attempt to pair the device.
4. **Restart your phone**: If the Bluetooth connection still doesn't work, restarting your phone can often solve the issue.
5. **Clear Bluetooth cache**: Go to **Settings > Apps & Notifications > See All Apps > Bluetooth** and clear the cache to resolve any software issues.

Use Google Meet for Video Calls

In today's world, **video calls** are becoming increasingly important. Whether for work, catching up with friends and family, or attending online meetings, **Google Meet** is a powerful tool that allows you to make video calls on your **Pixel 9 Pro**. Let's go over how to set up and use **Google Meet**.

Step 1: Install Google Meet

If **Google Meet** is not already installed on your phone, you can easily download it from the **Google Play Store**.

1. **Open the Google Play Store**:

    ○ Tap on the **Google Play Store** icon from your **Home Screen** or **App Drawer**.

2. **Search for Google Meet**:

   ○ In the **Play Store**, tap on the search bar
     at the top and type in **Google Meet**.

3. **Install the App**:

   ○ Tap **Install** to download and install the
     app on your **Pixel 9 Pro**.

Step 2: Set Up Google Meet

Once you have installed **Google Meet**, you need to set
it up:

1. **Open the Google Meet App**:

   ○ Tap the **Google Meet** icon to open the
     app.

2. **Sign In with Google Account**:

   ○ You will be prompted to sign in with your
     Google Account. Enter your Google
     credentials (email and password) to sign
     in. If you don't have a Google account,
     you will need to create one.

3. **Set Up Google Meet**:

   ○ After signing in, you will be able to set up
     your profile and customize the app's
     settings. You can adjust the microphone

and camera settings, and make sure everything is ready for video calls.

Step 3: Make a Video Call

Making a video call with **Google Meet** is easy:

1. **Tap on New Meeting**:

   o On the main screen of **Google Meet**, tap on the **New Meeting** button to start a new call.

2. **Invite People**:

   o You can invite people by sharing a link to the meeting or by sending an invitation through **email** or **calendar**.

3. **Join a Meeting**:

   o If you've received an invitation to a meeting, tap on the **Join Meeting** button and enter the meeting code or click on the link in the invitation.

4. **Start the Video Call**:

   o Once everyone has joined the meeting, you can start the video call. You will be able to see everyone's video feed and use the microphone and camera to communicate.

5. **End the Call**:

   ○ To leave the call, tap the red **Leave Call** button at the bottom of the screen.

Step 4: Adjust Google Meet Settings

During a call, you can adjust the following settings:

- **Mute/Unmute Microphone**: Tap the microphone icon to mute or unmute your mic.
- **Turn Camera On/Off**: Tap the camera icon to toggle your video feed on or off.
- **Share Screen**: If you want to share something on your screen, tap the **Share Screen** button to show documents, presentations, or apps during the call.

Enable Satellite SOS (USA Only)

In case of an emergency, **Satellite SOS** can help you communicate when you're in an area without regular cell service. This feature is available on your **Google Pixel 9 Pro** for emergency situations, allowing you to send SOS messages via satellite.

Here's how to set up **Satellite SOS** on your **Pixel 9 Pro**:

Step 1: Open the Settings App

1. **Go to Settings**:

     ○ Tap the **Settings** icon from your **Home Screen** or **App Drawer** to open the **Settings** menu.
2. **Scroll to Safety & Emergency**:

     ○ Scroll down and tap on **Safety & Emergency** in the **Settings** menu. This section contains emergency features like **Emergency Alerts** and **Satellite SOS**.

Step 2: Set Up Satellite SOS

1. **Enable Satellite SOS**:

     ○ In the **Safety & Emergency** section, look for **Satellite SOS**. Follow the on-screen instructions to enable this feature. You may need to grant permissions for location access and other emergency settings.
2. **Set Up Emergency Contact**:

     ○ Once **Satellite SOS** is enabled, set up your **emergency contact**. This is the person or group who will receive your SOS messages if you need help.

Step 3: Using Satellite SOS in an Emergency

If you find yourself in an emergency situation where you don't have regular cell service, you can use **Satellite SOS** to send a distress message. Here's how:

1. **Activate Satellite SOS**:

   ○ To activate **Satellite SOS**, press the **power button** and **volume up button** simultaneously (or follow the emergency steps on the screen).

2. **Send SOS Message**:

   ○ Once activated, **Satellite SOS** will use available satellite signals to send your emergency message. Your location and a brief message will be sent to your emergency contact, notifying them that you need help.

Conclusion

In this chapter, we covered the essential **communication and connectivity features** of your **Google Pixel 9 Pro**. You now know how to connect to **Wi-Fi** and **Bluetooth**, use **Google Meet** for video calls, and enable **Satellite SOS** for emergency communication. These features make it easier to stay connected and ensure you are always prepared in critical situations.

Your **Pixel 9 Pro** offers more than just standard communication—it helps you stay connected in smarter and safer ways. In the next chapters, we will continue exploring other features and tips to make your experience with the phone even better.

Chapter Nine

Security and Privacy on Your Google Pixel 9 Pro

In today's digital world, **security** and **privacy** are more important than ever. Your **Google Pixel 9 Pro** comes with a variety of built-in features designed to protect your information and keep your phone secure. From setting up **Face Unlock** and **Fingerprint Unlock** to managing **app permissions** and ensuring your **Google Play Protect** is active, this chapter will guide you through all the essential steps to secure your phone and manage your privacy settings.

By the end of this chapter, you'll have a good understanding of how to protect your device, your personal information, and ensure your apps are safe from harmful software.

Set Up Security Options

Security is the first line of defense in protecting your **Google Pixel 9 Pro** and the information stored on it. In this section, we will walk you through setting up strong **security options** like **Face Unlock, Fingerprint Unlock**, and **two-factor authentication** for your **Google Account**.

Step 1: Use Face Unlock or Fingerprint Unlock for Added Security

To keep your phone secure, you can set up **Face Unlock** or **Fingerprint Unlock**. These features use biometric data to ensure that only you can unlock your phone. Both of these options are fast, easy, and secure.

Setting Up Face Unlock

1. **Go to Settings**:

   - Open the **Settings** app on your **Pixel 9 Pro**.

2. **Select Security**:

   - Scroll down and tap on **Security** to open the security settings.

3. **Tap on Face Unlock**:

   - Under the **Security** settings, you will see **Face Unlock**. Tap on it to begin the setup.

4. **Follow the On-Screen Instructions**:

   - The phone will ask you to position your face in front of the camera. You will need to align your face within the frame on the screen. Make sure you are in a well-lit area to get an accurate scan.

- Once your face is registered, the phone will store the data and allow you to unlock your phone simply by looking at it.

5. **Set a Backup**:

   - It's recommended to set a **backup** in case Face Unlock fails or doesn't work in certain situations (like in low light). You can use a **PIN**, **password**, or **pattern** as a backup option.

Setting Up Fingerprint Unlock

If you prefer using your **fingerprint** for security, here's how to set it up:

1. **Go to Settings**:

   - Open the **Settings** app on your phone.

2. **Select Security**:

   - Tap on **Security** to open the security options.

3. **Tap on Fingerprint**:

   - Find the **Fingerprint** option and tap on it.

4. **Register Your Fingerprint**:

   - Follow the instructions to place your finger on the fingerprint sensor located on the **back** of your **Pixel 9 Pro**. You will need to place your finger on the sensor multiple times from different angles to ensure a complete scan.

5. **Set a Backup Option**:

    ○ Like with **Face Unlock**, it's important to set a **backup PIN**, **password**, or **pattern** in case the fingerprint sensor is not available or doesn't work properly.

Step 2: Enable Two-Factor Authentication for Your Google Account

Two-factor authentication (2FA) adds an extra layer of security to your **Google Account** by requiring you to enter both your password and a second code sent to your phone. This ensures that even if someone has your password, they cannot access your account without the second factor.

To set up **two-factor authentication** for your **Google Account**, follow these steps:

1. **Go to Settings**:

    ○ Open the **Settings** app on your **Pixel 9 Pro**.

2. **Tap on Google**:

    ○ Scroll down and tap on **Google** to open your **Google Account** settings.

3. **Select Security**:

   ○ Tap on **Security** under your **Google Account** settings.

4. **Tap on Two-Step Verification**:

   ○ Scroll down to **Two-Step Verification** and tap on it. If prompted, sign in to your **Google Account**.

5. **Follow the On-Screen Instructions**:

   ○ Google will guide you through the process of setting up **two-factor authentication**. You will need to choose how you want to receive your second factor. You can choose from options like:
      ■ **Text Message**: A code will be sent to your phone via SMS.
      ■ **Google Authenticator**: An app that generates a code for you.
      ■ **Google Prompt**: Google will send a notification to your phone, and you just need to tap **Yes** to confirm your identity.

6. **Complete Setup**:

   ○ Once you choose your second factor, Google will confirm that **two-factor authentication** is active and will provide backup options in case you lose access to your phone.

Now, your **Google Account** is more secure, as it requires both your password and the second factor to sign in.

Privacy Settings

Your **privacy** is just as important as your phone's security. The **Pixel 9 Pro** offers several **privacy settings** that let you control what information is shared and with whom. In this section, we will show you how to manage app permissions, location settings, and control which apps can access your personal data.

Step 1: Manage App Permissions

Apps often ask for permission to access your phone's features, like the **camera**, **location**, or **contacts**. You can control which apps have access to these features and adjust their permissions at any time.

1. **Open the Settings App**:

    ○ Tap the **Settings** icon from your **Home Screen** or **App Drawer** to open **Settings**.
2. **Select Privacy**:

    ○ Scroll down and tap on **Privacy**.
3. **Tap on Permission Manager**:

- In the **Privacy** section, tap on **Permission Manager**. This will show a list of all the permissions available on your phone, such as **Camera**, **Location**, **Microphone**, and **Storage**.

4. **Select a Permission Type**:

   - For example, if you want to manage which apps have access to your **location**, tap on **Location**. You will see a list of apps that have requested access to your location.

5. **Adjust App Permissions**:

   - Tap on any app in the list to change its permission. You can choose from:
     - **Allow**: The app can access the selected data.
     - **Deny**: The app cannot access the selected data.
     - **Ask Every Time**: The app will ask you each time it needs access to that data.

6. **Repeat for Other Permissions**:

   - You can repeat these steps for other permissions, such as **Camera**, **Microphone**, **Contacts**, and **Storage**.

Step 2: Enable Location History and Activity Controls

For a more personalized experience, **Google** offers **Location History** and **Activity Controls**. These features allow Google to track your location and activity across services like **Google Maps** and **Google Search**, helping you receive personalized recommendations and search results.

1. **Go to Settings**:

   ○ Open the **Settings** app on your phone.
2. **Tap on Google**:

   ○ Scroll down and tap on **Google**.
3. **Select Location**:

   ○ In the **Google** section, tap on **Location** to access location-related settings.
4. **Enable Location History**:

   ○ Toggle the switch to enable **Location History**. This will allow Google to track the places you visit and improve services like **Google Maps**.
5. **Adjust Activity Controls**:

   ○ Under **Activity Controls**, you can manage **Web & App Activity**, **YouTube History**, and **Location History**. You can turn off these features at any time if you prefer not to have your data tracked.

6. **Review and Delete Activity**:

   ○ You can review and delete your activity
     by visiting the **My Activity** page in the
     Google app or on the web.

Google Play Protect

Google Play Protect is a built-in security feature that
helps protect your **Pixel 9 Pro** from harmful apps. It
scans your apps and other content for potential security
risks and warns you if anything suspicious is found.

Step 1: Ensure Google Play Protect is Enabled

1. **Open the Settings App**:

   ○ Open the **Settings** app on your **Pixel 9
     Pro**.
2. **Tap on Google**:

   ○ Scroll down and tap on **Google** in the
     Settings menu.
3. **Select Play Protect**:

   ○ In the **Google** section, tap on **Play
     Protect**. This will open the **Google Play
     Protect** settings.

4. **Turn On Play Protect**:

   - Make sure the **Play Protect** option is toggled on. When enabled, **Play Protect** will automatically scan apps on your phone for harmful behavior.
5. **Scan for Harmful Apps**:

   - You can manually scan your phone for harmful apps by tapping **Scan**. If any harmful apps are found, **Google Play Protect** will notify you and suggest removing them.

Step 2: View Play Protect Alerts

If **Google Play Protect** finds any potential security risks or harmful apps, it will send you a notification. You can also check for alerts within the **Play Protect** section of your **Google Settings**.

Conclusion

In this chapter, we've covered how to secure your **Google Pixel 9 Pro** by setting up strong security options, such as **Face Unlock, Fingerprint Unlock**, and **two-factor authentication** for your **Google Account**. We also explored how to manage your **privacy settings**, control app permissions, and enable **Location**

History and **Activity Controls** to create a personalized experience. Additionally, we discussed **Google Play Protect**, which helps keep your phone safe from harmful apps.

By following the steps in this chapter, you can make sure that your phone remains secure and your personal data is protected. In the next chapters, we will continue exploring other advanced features and settings to optimize your **Google Pixel 9 Pro**.

Chapter Ten

Advanced Features and Tips for Your Google Pixel 9 Pro

In this chapter, we will explore the **advanced features** and tips that can enhance your experience with the **Google Pixel 9 Pro**. From **hidden features** and **customization options** to powerful **camera tools** and efficient **battery management**, we will show you how to get the most out of your phone. We'll also dive into features like **Google Lens** and **Live Translate**, which offer unique ways to interact with the world around you.

By the end of this chapter, you will be equipped with the knowledge to use your **Pixel 9 Pro** to its fullest potential.

Hidden Features and Customization Options

Your **Google Pixel 9 Pro** is filled with **hidden features** and **customization options** that aren't immediately obvious. These features can help you personalize your phone and make it even easier to use. Let's go through some of the hidden options and tips that will make your phone more unique to you.

1. Gesture Navigation

One of the **hidden features** of Android 14 is the ability to use **gesture navigation**. Instead of relying on the traditional **navigation buttons** (Back, Home, and Recent), you can control your **Pixel 9 Pro** with simple swipes and gestures. This gives you more screen space and a smoother, more fluid experience.

How to Enable Gesture Navigation:

1. **Open Settings**:

   - Tap the **Settings** icon on your **Home Screen** or **App Drawer**.

2. **Go to System**:

   - Scroll down and tap on **System**.

3. **Select Gestures**:

   - In the **System** section, tap on **Gestures** to open the gesture settings.

4. **Enable Gesture Navigation**:

   - Tap on **System Navigation** and choose **Gesture Navigation**. This will enable the **gestures** on your phone. Now, you can swipe up to go home, swipe left or right to switch between apps, and swipe down for the notification panel.

Why Use Gesture Navigation?

- Gesture navigation gives you a cleaner look and a more immersive experience. It also saves space by eliminating on-screen buttons, allowing you to make better use of your phone's display.

2. Digital Wellbeing & Focus Mode

If you're looking to reduce distractions and focus more on your work or personal life, **Digital Wellbeing** is a fantastic feature. It lets you track your phone usage and set **screen time limits** for individual apps. You can also use **Focus Mode** to silence apps temporarily, helping you stay focused.

How to Set Up Focus Mode:

1. **Go to Settings**:

   - Open the **Settings** app.
2. **Select Digital Wellbeing & Parental Controls**:

   - Tap on **Digital Wellbeing**.
3. **Enable Focus Mode**:

   - In the **Digital Wellbeing** menu, tap on **Focus Mode** and select the apps you want to silence.
4. **Start Focus Mode**:

   - Once you've selected the apps to silence, turn on **Focus Mode**. This will temporarily stop the notifications from those apps, allowing you to focus without distractions.

3. Customizing the Quick Settings Menu

The **Quick Settings** menu is a useful feature on your **Pixel 9 Pro**, giving you quick access to settings like **Wi-Fi**, **Bluetooth**, and **Do Not Disturb**. You can customize this menu to make it even more efficient for your needs.

How to Customize Quick Settings:

1. **Swipe Down the Notification Panel**:

   o Swipe down from the top of your screen to open the **Quick Settings** panel.
2. **Tap on the Edit Icon**:

   o Tap the **edit icon** (it looks like a pencil) at the bottom-left corner of the **Quick Settings** menu.
3. **Rearrange the Tiles**:

   o In **edit mode**, you can drag and drop tiles to rearrange them. For example, you can move the **Battery Saver** tile to the top for quick access, or add new tiles for features you use frequently.

4. **Add New Tiles**:

   - You can also tap **Add** to add new tiles for options like **Screen Record, Do Not Disturb**, or **Location**.

Advanced Camera Tips

The **Google Pixel 9 Pro** comes with a powerful **camera system** that includes several **AI-powered tools** and **advanced settings** to help you take stunning photos and videos. In this section, we'll walk you through some of the more advanced **camera features** that can elevate your photography game.

1. Super Res Zoom

Super Res Zoom is a feature that uses **AI** to enhance the quality of zoomed-in photos. Unlike traditional zoom, which can result in blurry images, **Super Res Zoom** keeps your photos sharp, even when zooming in up to 5x.

How to Use Super Res Zoom:

1. **Open the Camera App**:

   - Tap on the **Camera app** from your **Home Screen**.

2. **Select the Zoom Slider**:

   o In the **Camera app**, you will see a **zoom slider**. Slide it to zoom in on the subject.
3. **Use Super Res Zoom**:

   o The **Pixel 9 Pro** will automatically apply **Super Res Zoom** when you zoom in beyond the optical zoom limit (typically 2x). You can continue zooming up to 5x while keeping your image sharp and clear.

Why Use Super Res Zoom?

• **Super Res Zoom** allows you to capture distant subjects with greater detail. Whether you're photographing wildlife or a faraway landmark, you can zoom in without losing image quality.

2. AI Tools for Enhancing Photos

The **Pixel 9 Pro** has several **AI-powered camera tools** that automatically enhance your photos. These tools include **Auto Enhance, Night Sight**, and **Portrait Mode**, which improve lighting, focus, and clarity in your images.

How to Use AI Tools:

1. **Auto Enhance**:

- Auto Enhance is enabled by default. When you take a photo, the **Pixel 9 Pro** will automatically adjust brightness, contrast, and color for the best result. You don't need to do anything—just take the photo, and the AI will handle the rest.

2. **Night Sight**:

- **Night Sight** is perfect for taking clear photos in low-light conditions. To use it, open the **Camera app**, swipe to **Night Sight**, and take a picture in dim lighting. The camera will brighten the image and reduce noise.

3. **Portrait Mode**:

- To take professional-looking portraits, use **Portrait Mode**. This mode uses AI to blur the background, giving your subject a stunning bokeh effect. Simply select **Portrait Mode** from the camera app and focus on your subject.

Maximizing Battery and Performance

To get the most out of your **Google Pixel 9 Pro**, it's important to optimize both **battery life** and **performance**. Android 14 has several features that help you extend battery life, while also making sure that your phone stays fast and efficient.

1. Battery Saver and Extreme Battery Saver

Battery Saver helps you conserve energy by limiting background processes, reducing screen brightness, and turning off non-essential features. **Extreme Battery Saver** goes even further, ensuring that your phone lasts as long as possible by turning off most background apps and services.

How to Enable Battery Saver:

1. **Open Settings**:

   - Tap the **Settings** icon on your **Home Screen**.
2. **Go to Battery**:

   - Tap on **Battery** to open battery-related settings.
3. **Turn On Battery Saver**:

   - Tap on **Battery Saver** and toggle it on to reduce power consumption.

How to Enable Extreme Battery Saver:

1. **Open Settings**:

   - Tap **Settings** and then **Battery**.

2. **Enable Extreme Battery Saver**:

    ○ Tap on **Extreme Battery Saver** and turn
       it on to extend battery life for up to **72
       hours** by limiting background apps and
       services.

2. Performance Boost with Developer Options

If you want to make your **Pixel 9 Pro** run faster, you can
use the **Developer Options** menu to tweak
performance settings, including **animation speeds** and
background processes.

How to Enable Developer Options:

1. **Open Settings**:

    ○ Go to **Settings** on your phone.
2. **Go to About Phone**:

    ○ Scroll down and tap on **About Phone**.
3. **Tap Build Number**:

    ○ Tap the **Build Number** seven times to
       enable **Developer Options**.

Adjust Performance Settings:

1. **Go to Developer Options**:

- In **Settings**, tap **System** and then **Developer Options**.
2. **Disable or Speed Up Animations**:

- In **Developer Options**, you'll see settings like **Window Animation Scale** and **Transition Animation Scale**. Set them to **0.5x** or **Off** to speed up transitions and make the phone feel faster.

Using Google Lens and Live Translate

Your **Pixel 9 Pro** comes with powerful **AI** tools like **Google Lens** and **Live Translate** that make interacting with the world around you easier. **Google Lens** can recognize objects, text, and landmarks, while **Live Translate** lets you communicate in different languages in real-time.

1. Using Google Lens

Google Lens allows you to interact with the world around you by simply pointing your camera at objects. It can identify plants, animals, landmarks, and even scan text for translation or copying.

How to Use Google Lens:

1. **Open Google Lens**:

- Open the **Camera app** and tap the **Lens icon**. Alternatively, you can access **Google Lens** via the **Google Assistant** by saying, "Hey Google, use Lens."

2. **Point Your Camera at an Object**:

- Point your camera at an object, text, or a barcode. **Google Lens** will analyze the image and provide information, such as identifying objects, translating text, or providing shopping suggestions.

2. Using Live Translate

Live Translate allows you to have conversations in different languages in real-time. It's a great tool when traveling or communicating with someone who speaks a different language.

How to Use Live Translate:

1. **Open Google Translate**:

- Open the **Google Translate** app on your **Pixel 9 Pro**.

2. **Select Conversation Mode**:

- Tap on **Conversation Mode** to enable **Live Translate**. You can then speak to the phone in your language, and it will translate and speak the translation in the other person's language.

Conclusion

In this chapter, we explored **advanced features** and tips that will help you make the most of your **Google Pixel 9 Pro**. From using **Super Res Zoom** and **AI tools** for stunning photos to managing your **battery** and boosting **performance**, there are many ways to optimize your phone's capabilities. Additionally, we discussed how to use **Google Lens** and **Live Translate** for real-time object recognition and language translation, which enhances your phone's functionality even further.

With the knowledge gained from this chapter, you can now use your **Pixel 9 Pro** more effectively, making it an even more powerful tool for both daily tasks and creative endeavors. In the next chapters, we will continue exploring more features and settings to enhance your experience with the **Google Pixel 9 Pro**.

Chapter Eleven

Troubleshooting and FAQs for Your Google Pixel 9 Pro

Even though the **Google Pixel 9 Pro** is a powerful and reliable device, there are times when you might encounter small issues or have questions about how to make the most of its features. In this chapter, we will help you resolve common problems such as **Wi-Fi**, **Bluetooth**, and **camera issues**, as well as guide you on how to restore your device to **factory settings** if needed. We will also cover how to fix **battery and charging problems** and answer some frequently asked questions (FAQs) that many users have.

By the end of this chapter, you will be well-equipped to handle any issues that may arise with your **Google Pixel 9 Pro**, and you will have a better understanding of how to troubleshoot and resolve them.

Resolving Common Issues (Wi-Fi, Bluetooth, Camera)

Sometimes, your **Google Pixel 9 Pro** might experience issues with **Wi-Fi**, **Bluetooth**, or the **camera**. These are common problems that can often be solved with simple steps. Let's explore how to troubleshoot and fix each of these issues.

1. Resolving Wi-Fi Issues

Wi-Fi is essential for internet access, and a poor connection can make using your phone frustrating. If you're having trouble connecting to Wi-Fi or experiencing slow speeds, follow these steps to resolve the issue.

Step 1: Check Wi-Fi Settings

1. **Open the Settings App**:

   - Tap the **Settings** icon on your **Home Screen** or **App Drawer** to open the **Settings** menu.
2. **Go to Wi-Fi Settings**:

   - Tap on **Wi-Fi** and make sure Wi-Fi is turned on.
3. **Forget and Reconnect to the Network**:

   - If you are having trouble with a specific Wi-Fi network, tap on the network name and select **Forget**. Then, reconnect by selecting the network again and entering the password.

Step 2: Restart Your Phone

Sometimes, simply restarting your phone can resolve Wi-Fi issues. Hold the **Power button**, and then select **Restart** to reboot your phone.

Step 3: Restart Your Router

If your **Pixel 9 Pro** is still not connecting or has slow speeds, try restarting your **Wi-Fi router**. Unplug the router for about 10 seconds, then plug it back in. After the router restarts, try connecting to the Wi-Fi network again.

Step 4: Check for Interference

Sometimes, other devices or objects can cause interference with your Wi-Fi signal. Try moving closer to the router or removing any obstacles between your phone and the router to improve the connection.

2. Resolving Bluetooth Issues

Bluetooth lets you connect to other devices wirelessly, but sometimes it may not connect or experience issues with pairing. Here's how to troubleshoot and fix common Bluetooth problems.

Step 1: Check Bluetooth Settings

1. **Go to Settings**:

   ○ Open the **Settings** app on your phone.

2. **Select Bluetooth**:

   ○ Tap on **Bluetooth** and make sure it is
      turned on.

3. **Forget and Reconnect to the Device**:

   ○ If you are having trouble connecting to a
      specific Bluetooth device, tap on the
      device name and select **Forget**. Then,
      reconnect by selecting the device again.

Step 2: Restart Bluetooth

1. **Turn Bluetooth Off and On**:

   ○ Turn off **Bluetooth** by toggling the switch
      in the **Bluetooth** settings. Wait for a few
      seconds and then turn it back on.

2. **Restart Your Phone**:

   ○ Sometimes, restarting your phone can
      solve Bluetooth issues. Hold the **Power
      button**, and tap **Restart**.

Step 3: Check for Interference

Bluetooth devices can sometimes experience
interference from other devices that use similar
frequencies. Make sure that there are no other devices
nearby that could be causing this issue. Try moving to a
different location or turning off other devices that may
interfere with the Bluetooth connection.

Step 4: Update Software

Outdated software can sometimes cause connectivity issues. Check if there are any available updates for your **Google Pixel 9 Pro** by going to **Settings > System > Software Update**.

---

3. Resolving Camera Issues

The **camera** on your **Google Pixel 9 Pro** is one of its standout features, but sometimes you may encounter problems such as blurry images, camera crashes, or difficulties with focusing.

Step 1: Restart the Camera App

1. **Close the Camera App**:

    o   If the **camera app** is frozen or not working properly, close it by tapping the **Recent Apps** button and swiping the camera app off the screen.
2. **Reopen the Camera App**:

    o   After closing the app, reopen it and check if the issue is resolved.

Step 2: Clear Camera App Cache

1. **Go to Settings**:

   - Open the **Settings** app on your phone.
2. **Select Apps & Notifications**:

   - Tap on **Apps & Notifications**, then **See All Apps**.
3. **Find Camera App**:

   - Scroll through the list and tap on the **Camera app**.
4. **Clear Cache**:

   - Tap **Storage & Cache**, then tap **Clear Cache**. This will remove temporary files that might be causing issues with the camera.

Step 3: Update the Camera App

Ensure that the **Camera app** is up-to-date by checking for updates in the **Google Play Store**. Open the **Play Store**, search for the **Camera app**, and tap **Update** if there is a newer version available.

Step 4: Check for Software Updates

Sometimes, issues with the **camera** are resolved in **system updates**. Make sure that your phone is up to date by going to **Settings > System > Software Update**.

Restoring Your Device to Factory Settings

If you are experiencing persistent issues with your **Pixel 9 Pro** or want to erase all your personal data before selling or giving away the phone, you can restore it to **factory settings**. This will wipe all apps, files, and settings from the device and return it to its original state.

Step 1: Backup Your Data

Before performing a **factory reset**, it's important to back up all of your important data, such as photos, videos, and contacts, so you can restore them later.

You can back up your data to **Google Drive** or **Google Photos**:

- **Google Photos**: Back up photos and videos by opening the **Google Photos** app and turning on **Backup & Sync**.
- **Google Drive**: Go to **Settings > Google > Backup** to back up your app data, call history, contacts, and more.

Step 2: Factory Reset Your Phone

1. **Go to Settings**:

   - Open the **Settings** app on your phone.

2. **Select System**:

   o Scroll down and tap **System**.
3. **Tap Reset Options**:

   o In the **System** menu, tap **Reset Options**.
4. **Tap Erase All Data (Factory Reset)**:

   o Select **Erase All Data** (Factory Reset), and confirm by tapping **Erase All Data** again.
5. **Enter PIN or Password**:

   o You may be asked to enter your PIN, password, or pattern to confirm that you want to perform a factory reset.
6. **Wait for the Reset**:

   o Your phone will reset and restart. This process may take several minutes. Once complete, your **Google Pixel 9 Pro** will be restored to its original factory settings.

Step 3: Restore Your Data

Once the phone has been reset, you can set it up as new or restore your backed-up data. Follow the on-screen instructions to sign in to your **Google Account** and restore your files, apps, and settings.

Solving Battery and Charging Issues

If you are having trouble with your **battery** or **charging**, don't worry. These are common issues that can often be solved with a few simple steps. Here's how to troubleshoot and fix common **battery and charging problems**.

Step 1: Check the Charging Cable and Adapter

1. **Inspect the Cable**:

   - Make sure your **charging cable** is not damaged. If the cable is frayed or broken, replace it with a new one.

2. **Check the Charging Adapter**:

   - Sometimes, the issue could be with the **charging adapter**. Make sure the adapter is working properly and is plugged into a functional power outlet.

Step 2: Clean the Charging Port

Dirt or debris in the **charging port** can prevent your phone from charging properly. Here's how to clean it:

1. **Turn off the Phone**:

   - Power off your **Pixel 9 Pro** to avoid any damage while cleaning.

2. **Use Compressed Air**:

    ○ Use a can of compressed air to blow out any dust or debris from the charging port.
3. **Use a Toothpick or Soft Brush**:

    ○ If needed, use a toothpick or a soft brush to gently remove any remaining dirt from the charging port.

Step 3: Restart Your Phone

Sometimes, restarting your phone can fix charging or battery-related issues. Hold the **Power button** and tap **Restart** to reboot your phone.

Step 4: Check Battery Health

If your battery drains too quickly or isn't charging properly, it could be a sign of an issue with the battery itself. You can check the **battery health** using third-party apps or by contacting **Google support** for a battery diagnosis.

Answering Frequently Asked Questions (FAQs)

Q1: How can I speed up my Pixel 9 Pro?

You can speed up your phone by:

- **Clearing cached data**: Go to **Settings > Storage > Cached Data** and clear any temporary files.
- **Disabling unused apps**: Go to **Settings > Apps & Notifications** to disable apps you don't use.
- **Turning off animations**: Enable **Developer Options** and reduce or turn off **window** and **transition animations**.

Q2: How can I extend my Pixel 9 Pro's battery life?

To extend battery life, you can:

- Use **Battery Saver** mode.
- Enable **Adaptive Battery** in **Settings > Battery**.
- Lower the screen brightness or enable **Night Mode**.

Q3: My Pixel 9 Pro is overheating. What should I do?

If your phone is overheating:

- Make sure you are not running too many apps or playing demanding games.
- Turn off **background apps** and close unused apps.
- If the issue persists, remove any case or cover that may be trapping heat, and allow your phone to cool down.

Q4: How can I get rid of bloatware (pre-installed apps)?

You can **disable** apps that you don't use. Go to **Settings > Apps & Notifications > See All Apps**, select the app, and tap **Disable**.

Conclusion

In this chapter, we covered how to troubleshoot and resolve common issues such as **Wi-Fi, Bluetooth, camera problems**, and more. We also explained how to **restore your device to factory settings, solve battery and charging issues**, and answered some of the most frequently asked questions about your **Google Pixel 9 Pro**.

By following the steps outlined in this chapter, you should be able to address most problems you encounter with your **Pixel 9 Pro** and keep it running smoothly. If problems persist, don't hesitate to contact **Google Support** for further assistance.

We hope this chapter helps you get the most out of your **Google Pixel 9 Pro**.

Chapter Twelve

Accessories and Maintenance for Your Google Pixel 9 Pro

Your **Google Pixel 9 Pro** is a powerful and sleek device, and to ensure it stays in good condition and continues to perform at its best, it's essential to take care of it and make the right accessories available. In this chapter, we will discuss the **recommended accessories** for your **Pixel 9 Pro**, how to **care for your device**, and how to keep it running smoothly with **maintenance tips**. Additionally, we will cover how to get the most out of **Google Support** if you encounter any issues.

Let's begin by looking at some accessories that will help protect your **Pixel 9 Pro**, followed by tips for keeping your device in top shape.

Recommended Accessories for Your Pixel 9 Pro

Accessories enhance the experience of using your **Google Pixel 9 Pro**, offering protection, convenience, and better performance. The following accessories are some of the best options for getting the most out of your phone while ensuring it stays safe and secure.

1. Protective Case

A **protective case** is one of the most important accessories you can invest in for your **Pixel 9 Pro**. It helps prevent damage from accidental drops, bumps, and scratches. There are many types of cases, each offering different levels of protection and style.

Types of Protective Cases:

- **Slim Cases**: These cases provide a thin layer of protection without adding much bulk. They are a good choice if you want to keep the sleek look of your phone while offering minimal protection against scratches and light bumps.

- **Heavy-Duty Cases**: If you're worried about dropping your phone frequently or need extra protection, **heavy-duty cases** are a great option. These cases often feature reinforced corners, shock absorption, and rugged materials like rubber or plastic.

- **Wallet Cases**: A **wallet case** is a good choice if you prefer to carry your credit cards, ID, and cash in one place. These cases usually flip open and feature slots for cards, making them a convenient accessory for people who prefer a minimalist approach to carrying their essentials.

- **Clear Cases**: If you want to show off your **Pixel 9 Pro's design**, a **clear case** can offer protection while letting the phone's color and design show through. They are lightweight and offer moderate protection against scratches and minor drops.

How to Choose the Right Case:

- Consider the level of protection you need: Are you prone to dropping your phone or do you want just light protection?
- Think about the style: Do you prefer a sleek, slim case, or a rugged, heavy-duty option?
- Consider functionality: Do you want a case that doubles as a wallet or offers extra grip?

2. Screen Protector

A **screen protector** is a thin layer of film or glass that you place on the screen of your phone. It acts as a barrier between your phone's display and any potential scratches, cracks, or fingerprints.

Types of Screen Protectors:

- **Plastic Film Protectors**: These are thin layers of plastic that provide basic protection against scratches. They are less expensive than glass protectors but offer less protection from drops.

- **Tempered Glass Protectors**: **Tempered glass protectors** are stronger and provide better protection than plastic film. They offer excellent protection against scratches and impacts, and some even have special coatings to prevent smudges and fingerprints.

Why You Need a Screen Protector:

- **Protection Against Scratches**: Without a screen protector, your phone's display is more prone to scratches from everyday items like keys, coins, and even dust particles.
- **Prevents Cracks**: While a screen protector won't prevent a drop from cracking the screen, it can absorb some of the impact, reducing the likelihood of major damage.
- **Maintains Clarity**: **Tempered glass screen protectors** are often crystal clear, so they won't affect the clarity or touch sensitivity of the screen.

3. Wireless Charger

A **wireless charger** is a convenient way to charge your **Pixel 9 Pro** without needing to plug in a cable. Simply place your phone on the charging pad, and it will start charging automatically.

Benefits of Wireless Charging:

- **Convenience**: No need to plug and unplug cables. Just place your phone on the charger, and it will begin charging.
- **Clean Look**: Wireless chargers are great for keeping your workspace tidy and free of clutter from charging cables.
- **Compatibility**: Your **Pixel 9 Pro** supports **Qi wireless charging**, which means it is compatible with most wireless charging pads on the market.

Choosing the Right Wireless Charger:

- Look for a **fast wireless charger** that supports **fast charging** for your phone. **Google Pixel 9 Pro** supports up to **18W** wireless charging for quick power-ups.
- Consider a **wireless charging stand** if you prefer to keep your phone upright while charging for easier viewing during calls or video watching.

4. Bluetooth Headphones or Speakers

Since **Google Pixel 9 Pro** does not have a headphone jack, **Bluetooth headphones** or **Bluetooth speakers** are essential accessories if you enjoy listening to music or taking calls hands-free.

Why You Should Use Bluetooth Audio Devices:

- **Convenience**: No cables to deal with! Simply pair your phone with your Bluetooth headphones or speaker and enjoy music, podcasts, or videos.

- **Sound Quality**: Many **Bluetooth headphones** offer high-quality sound and noise cancellation, improving your listening experience.
- **Hands-Free Calling**: Bluetooth headsets make it easy to take calls while driving or working out.

Popular Bluetooth Accessories:

- **Bluetooth Headphones**: These come in various styles, including **over-ear**, **in-ear**, and **sports headphones**.
- **Bluetooth Speakers**: A portable Bluetooth speaker allows you to enjoy music outdoors or at home without using any cables.

Caring for Your Device: Case, Screen Protector, and Cleaning

To keep your **Google Pixel 9 Pro** in excellent condition, it's essential to care for the device regularly. Proper **cleaning**, using a **protective case**, and keeping a **screen protector** on the phone will help maintain its appearance and functionality.

1. Cleaning Your Pixel 9 Pro

Your **Google Pixel 9 Pro** should be cleaned regularly to maintain its appearance and ensure that the **screen**,

camera lenses, and **charging port** stay free from dust and dirt.

How to Clean Your Pixel 9 Pro:

1. **Turn Off Your Phone**:

    - Before cleaning, turn off your phone to avoid accidental touch inputs.

2. **Use a Microfiber Cloth**:

    - Use a **microfiber cloth** to clean the screen and body of your phone. Microfiber is soft and gentle, so it won't scratch the surface.

3. **Clean the Camera Lenses**:

    - To keep your camera lenses clear, use a soft cloth or lens cleaning cloth to wipe off fingerprints or dust.

4. **Avoid Harsh Chemicals**:

    - Don't use cleaning sprays or harsh chemicals on your phone. These can damage the screen or the finish on your phone. Stick to water and a soft cloth for cleaning.

5. **Clean the Charging Port**:

    - To clean the **charging port**, use a dry brush or compressed air to gently remove any dust or debris that may have accumulated.

2. Using a Case and Screen Protector

To prevent scratches, cracks, and other damage, using a **protective case** and **screen protector** is essential.

- **Case**: A **case** will protect your phone from drops and bumps. A **good case** will also absorb the impact if the phone is dropped, minimizing damage to the device.
- **Screen Protector**: A **screen protector** helps protect the **display** from scratches and fingerprints. It adds an extra layer of defense against accidental drops.

3. Storing Your Pixel 9 Pro

When not in use, store your phone in a safe place, like a bag or a **phone stand**, where it is less likely to get scratched or damaged. Avoid leaving your phone in places where it could be exposed to extreme temperatures, like inside a hot car, as this can affect the battery life and performance.

Software and Hardware Maintenance Tips

To ensure your **Pixel 9 Pro** continues to perform well over time, it's important to regularly maintain both its **software** and **hardware**.

1. Software Maintenance Tips

Keep Your Phone Updated:

- Regular **software updates** are important for the performance and security of your phone. To check for updates, go to **Settings > System > Software Update**.

Clear Cache and Unnecessary Files:

- Over time, your phone accumulates temporary files, which can slow down performance. To clear the cache, go to **Settings > Storage > Cached Data** and clear it to free up space.

Uninstall Unused Apps:

- If you have apps that you no longer use, it's a good idea to uninstall them. Go to **Settings > Apps & Notifications** to view and uninstall apps that are taking up unnecessary space.

2. Hardware Maintenance Tips

Check for Physical Damage:

- Regularly check your phone for any signs of physical damage. This includes cracks in the screen or damage to the charging port or camera lenses.

Battery Health:

- Over time, the battery health of your phone can degrade. To keep an eye on your **battery health**, go to **Settings > Battery** to see usage patterns. If you notice rapid battery drain, consider enabling **Battery Saver** or **Extreme Battery Saver**.

Getting the Most Out of Google Support

Even though your **Google Pixel 9 Pro** is a reliable device, you may encounter issues that need professional support. **Google Support** is there to help you solve any problems or answer any questions you might have.

1. Access Google Support

There are several ways you can get help from **Google Support**:

- **Visit the Google Support Website:**

- Go to **support.google.com** to find answers to common questions, troubleshooting tips, and solutions for any issues you may encounter.
- **Use the Google Support App**:

  - You can also use the **Google Support app** to get help. It offers instant support, chat features, and guides to help you solve any problems with your **Pixel 9 Pro**.

2. Contact Google Support

If you need more personalized assistance, you can contact **Google Support**:

- **Call Google Support**:

  - You can call **Google Support** directly to speak with a representative who can help you with issues related to your **Pixel 9 Pro**.
- **Use the Chat Feature**:

  - You can chat with a **Google Support** agent for quicker, real-time assistance.

Conclusion

In this chapter, we've covered how to maintain and protect your **Google Pixel 9 Pro** with the right **accessories**, such as a **case**, **screen protector**, and **wireless charger**. We've also shared tips for **cleaning your device**, maintaining **software and hardware**, and getting the most out of **Google Support** when needed. By following these simple steps and using the right accessories, you can ensure that your phone stays in excellent condition and continues to perform at its best.

Regular maintenance and care will help extend the life of your **Google Pixel 9 Pro** and keep it functioning smoothly for years to come. In the next chapters, we will continue exploring more ways to optimize your phone and troubleshoot any remaining issues.

Conclusion

Enjoying Your Google Pixel 9 Pro Experience

The **Google Pixel 9 Pro** is a sophisticated device designed to offer users an exceptional experience in terms of performance, photography, and ease of use. Throughout this guide, we've walked you through setting up, customizing, troubleshooting, and optimizing your phone to ensure you get the most out of its many features. In this conclusion, we will recap the **key features** and **tips** covered in this guide, provide information on where to get **additional help and support**, and discuss how to make the most of your **Pixel 9 Pro** experience.

Summary of Key Features and Tips

The **Google Pixel 9 Pro** is packed with a variety of features designed to make your everyday life easier, more efficient, and enjoyable. Let's quickly review the most important features and tips covered in this guide.

1. Security Features

Your **Pixel 9 Pro** offers several **security options** to protect your personal data:

- **Face Unlock** and **Fingerprint Unlock**: Use your face or fingerprint for quick and secure access to your phone.
- **Two-Factor Authentication**: Add an extra layer of security to your **Google Account** by enabling two-factor authentication.
- **Privacy Settings**: Control what apps can access your **location, camera**, and other sensitive data using the **Permission Manager**.

Tip: Always enable a **backup security method**, such as a **PIN, password**, or **pattern**, in case your biometric unlock methods fail.

2. Customization and Personalization

One of the best things about the **Pixel 9 Pro** is how easily you can customize it to match your preferences:

- **Themes and Wallpapers**: You can change the **theme** (Light or Dark) and set a **wallpaper** to reflect your personal style.
- **Widgets**: Add useful widgets like weather, calendar, and news directly to your **Home Screen** for easy access to important information.
- **Quick Settings**: Customize your **Quick Settings** menu to give you fast access to the tools and features you use most.

Tip: Make use of **gesture navigation** for a cleaner look and faster interaction with your phone.

3. Camera and AI Tools

The **camera system** on your **Pixel 9 Pro** is one of the standout features, offering AI-powered tools that enhance your photos automatically:

- **Super Res Zoom**: Allows you to zoom in up to 5x while maintaining sharpness and clarity.
- **AI Tools**: Tools like **Night Sight** for low-light photography and **Portrait Mode** for professional-looking pictures.
- **Google Photos Editing**: AI tools in **Google Photos** can automatically enhance your photos, adjust lighting, or suggest edits.

Tip: Try experimenting with **AI-powered editing** in **Google Photos** to take your images to the next level with just a few taps.

4. Connectivity and Communication

Staying connected is easy with the **Pixel 9 Pro**:

- **Wi-Fi and Bluetooth**: Quickly connect to Wi-Fi networks and Bluetooth devices for seamless communication and data transfer.
- **Google Meet**: Set up **Google Meet** for video calls and meetings with a few simple steps.
- **Satellite SOS**: In emergencies, use **Satellite SOS** (available in the USA) to send distress signals when cellular service is unavailable.

Tip: Regularly check your **Wi-Fi and Bluetooth settings** to ensure smooth connectivity with your devices.

5. Battery and Performance

Maximizing the **battery life** and **performance** of your **Pixel 9 Pro** ensures that you always have a reliable device at your disposal:

- **Battery Saver and Extreme Battery Saver**: Use these features to extend battery life when needed.
- **Developer Options**: Adjust performance settings, such as **animations**, to make your phone feel faster.
- **Performance Optimizations**: Clear app caches, disable unused apps, and enable **Adaptive Battery** for a smoother experience.

Tip: If your phone's battery is draining quickly, try turning off **background apps** and enabling **Battery Saver**.

6. Google Assistant and AI Features

Your **Pixel 9 Pro** features the **Google Assistant**, which is powered by AI to make tasks more efficient and hands-free:

- **Voice Commands**: Use **Google Assistant** to send texts, set reminders, check the weather,

and control your smart home devices with just your voice.
- **AI-Powered Tools**: Tools like **Google Lens** and **Live Translate** let you translate text in real time and identify objects around you.

Tip: Personalize **Google Assistant** to better serve your needs by setting up **Voice Match** and customizing the assistant's settings.

7. Privacy and Security Features

Protecting your **personal information** and **privacy** is key in today's world:

- **Location History** and **Activity Controls**: Track and manage what information is shared with Google services.
- **Google Play Protect**: Make sure **Google Play Protect** is enabled to scan your apps for harmful content.
- **App Permissions**: Use the **Permission Manager** to control which apps can access sensitive data like your location, camera, and contacts.

Tip: Regularly review your app permissions and ensure that apps only have access to the data they truly need.

8. Troubleshooting

The **Pixel 9 Pro** comes with troubleshooting tools to resolve issues like **Wi-Fi**, **Bluetooth**, and **camera** problems. If problems persist, consider restoring the device to **factory settings** or contacting **Google Support** for additional help.

Where to Get Additional Help and Support

Despite the **Google Pixel 9 Pro** being a highly reliable and feature-packed device, sometimes you might encounter issues or have questions. Fortunately, **Google** offers multiple ways to provide support and resolve any challenges you may face.

1. Google Support Website

The first place to check for help is the **Google Support website**. This site offers step-by-step guides, troubleshooting tips, and solutions for a wide variety of issues. You can search for topics related to your **Pixel 9 Pro** or browse popular help topics to find answers quickly.

How to Access Google Support:

1. Go to **support.google.com** using your browser.
2. Search for the issue or topic you need help with.
3. Follow the troubleshooting steps or guides to resolve the problem.

2. Google Support App

Another great resource is the **Google Support App**, which is available for download on the **Google Play Store**. This app provides quick access to live chat with Google support representatives, as well as troubleshooting tips and FAQs.

How to Use the Google Support App:

1. Download the **Google Support app** from the **Google Play Store**.
2. Open the app and search for the issue you need help with.
3. Follow the steps provided or connect with a support agent for personalized help.

3. Google Store Support

If you purchased your **Pixel 9 Pro** from the **Google Store**, you can contact **Google Store Support** for help with order-related issues, device exchanges, or warranty claims.

How to Contact Google Store Support:

1. Visit the **Google Store Support** page: **store.google.com**.
2. Look for contact options, such as **phone support** or **live chat**.
3. Follow the steps for resolving your issue, such as returning a device or checking warranty status.

4. Google Community Forums

Google also has **community forums** where users can post questions and share experiences. The forums are a good place to find solutions to common issues that others may have faced. You can read through existing threads or create a new one to ask for help.

How to Access the Google Community Forums:

1. Visit **support.google.com**.
2. Scroll down to **Community** and click on it.
3. Search for topics or ask your own question in the community forum.

5. Contacting Google Customer Support

If the above options don't resolve your issue, you can always contact **Google Customer Support** directly. They are available to assist you with advanced troubleshooting, hardware issues, or any other problems.

How to Contact Google Customer Support:

1. Go to **support.google.com** and navigate to the **Contact Us** section.
2. Choose **Phone**, **Chat**, or **Email** support based on your preference.
3. Follow the instructions to get in touch with a representative.

Enjoying Your Pixel 9 Pro Experience

Your **Google Pixel 9 Pro** offers a wealth of features designed to make your life easier, more productive, and more enjoyable. From **camera tools** that make photography simple to **AI-powered assistants** that can handle everyday tasks, your **Pixel 9 Pro** is packed with tools that make it a joy to use.

To get the most out of your phone, here are a few tips to enhance your experience:

1. **Stay Organized**: Use **app folders** and **widgets** to keep your **Home Screen** organized and easily accessible. Set up **gesture controls** to navigate your phone more efficiently.

2. **Optimize Battery Life**: Use **Battery Saver** and **Adaptive Battery** to make sure your phone lasts as long as possible throughout the day.

3. **Experiment with the Camera**: Try out the **AI camera features** like **Super Res Zoom**, **Night Sight**, and **Portrait Mode** to capture stunning photos in any setting.

4. **Take Advantage of Google Services**: Use **Google Assistant**, **Google Lens**, and **Google Photos** to access information, translate text, and

enhance your photos.

5. **Ensure Security**: Enable **two-factor authentication, Face Unlock**, and **Fingerprint Unlock** to keep your phone and personal information secure.

6. **Use Cloud Services**: Take advantage of **Google Drive, Google Photos**, and **Google One** to back up and store your important files, photos, and videos.

Conclusion

The **Google Pixel 9 Pro** is more than just a phone; it's a powerful device that integrates advanced **AI**, seamless **Google services**, and **cutting-edge hardware** to enhance your everyday life. Whether you're using it to capture stunning photos, stay organized, or manage your tasks, the **Pixel 9 Pro** is designed to make life easier.

We've covered everything from **setting up your phone** to **advanced camera tips, security features, privacy settings**, and **troubleshooting**. We hope this guide has helped you unlock the full potential of your **Pixel 9 Pro**.

Should you need additional help, don't hesitate to reach out to **Google Support** for assistance. Now, enjoy your **Pixel 9 Pro** and make the most of its incredible features!

www.ingramcontent.com/pod-product-compliance
Lightning Source LLC
LaVergne TN
LVHW051444050326
832903LV00030BD/3235